Thank you for picking up my book. Your support means a lot, and I hope you find the read both enjoyable and insightful. Beyond being an author, my work extends into research and consultancy within organizational behavior and leadership. I engage with a broad spectrum of clients, from individuals to larger teams and organizations, offering guidance in leadership development.

For a deeper dive into my professional background and consulting philosophy, several websites are available. There, you'll also find my contact details. I'm eager to hear your thoughts on the book or discuss potential collaboration in leadership coaching.

Discover more about my work and other publications related to leadership and organizational behavior at my personal website, https://thomaspatrickhuber.com.

Learn about my specific approach to leadership coaching and consulting at https://elevateus.ch, the official website of my company.

Lastly, in case you want to reach out to me directly please send me an email at thomaspatrick@mac.com.

I appreciate your support in purchasing this book and look forward to connecting with you.

Wishing you an enlightening journey,

Thomas P Huber, PhD, MS ECS

Introduction: Welcome to the Leadership Labyrinth

Imagine a cave, as depicted by the ancient philosopher Plato. In this cave, prisoners are chained, their gaze fixed upon a wall. Behind them, a fire burns, casting shadows on the wall from objects passed in front of it. These shadows represent the prisoners' perceived reality, yet they are mere illusions of the true forms behind them. This cave is a metaphor for the world of leadership. Many leaders are like these prisoners, chained to a limited understanding of what leadership entails. They see only the shadows. But there is a world outside this cave, a world where leadership is not just about power and control but about balance and empowerment.

Our journey in this book is akin to that of the prisoner who breaks free from the chains, emerging from the darkness of the cave into the light of the outside world. Just as the prisoner's eyes gradually adjust to the sunlight, revealing a reality far more vivid and detailed than the shadows, we will explore the depths and nuances of leadership. From the oppressive shadows of 'Darth Vader in a Suit', through the balanced pathway of 'Militant Neutrality', to the enlightening 'Gandhis of the Boardroom', we will navigate the labyrinth of leadership. Let this book be your guide out of the cave, into a world where leadership is not a shadowy illusion, but a tangible, transformative force. Welcome to the Leadership Labyrinth, where the journey from darkness to light begins.

In the realm of leadership, envision a vast spectrum. At one end lies the dark side: leadership marked by destructive behaviors, where manipulation, fear, and negativity reign. This is a realm where short-term gains overshadow long-term wellbeing, often leading to toxic environments. On the other end of the spectrum shines the light side: leadership that is inspiring, positive, and empowering. Here, leaders nurture growth, foster trust, and encourage innovation, creating environments where individuals and organizations flourish. This spectrum illustrates the diverse nature of leadership, encompassing a wide range of styles and impacts.

Leadership may be likened to a labyrinth, a fitting metaphor for its intricate nature. Like a labyrinth, the path of leadership is not linear but filled with complexities, twists, and turns. Each corridor represents different challenges and opportunities, decisions and consequences. Navigating this labyrinth requires not only skill and knowledge but also intuition and adaptability. Leaders must be prepared to encounter unexpected obstacles, to retrace their steps, and to find new pathways. This metaphor encapsulates the journey of leadership, one that is unpredictable and multifaceted, demanding both courage and wisdom to navigate successfully.

We begin our journey in the shadowy realms of leadership, a place where destructive behaviors cast a long, ominous shadow over the landscape of organizations and teams. This part of the book delves into the nature of destructive leadership – a style characterized by manipulation, coercion, and a disregard for the wellbeing of others. It's a world where communication is marred by deceit, decision-making by selfishness, and team dynamics by fear and mistrust. The repercussions of such leadership ripple through organizations, eroding morale, stifling innovation, and breeding a culture of discontent and dysfunction. As we navigate through these dark corridors, we'll explore how such leadership manifests, its impact on individuals and organizations, and the subtle, often insidious ways it can take root. This exploration sets the stage for understanding the critical need for transformation and the journey towards a more positive, constructive form of leadership.

Militant Neutrality, in the context of leadership, represents a stage of enlightenment and balance beyond the confines of the dark and labyrinthine aspects of leadership. It symbolizes a conscious choice to embrace fairness and empathy, standing firmly in a space that avoids extremes. This approach is about active engagement and thoughtful mediation, where decisions are made with a deep understanding of varying perspectives. Leaders who embody Militant Neutrality navigate the complexities of their roles with a focus on harmony, equity, and a keen awareness of the diverse needs and dynamics within their organizations.

As we step beyond the shadows and militant neutrality, we approach the realm of positive leadership. This section of the book will illuminate the qualities of positive, inspiring leaders who not only achieve organizational goals but also foster a culture of engagement, innovation, and well-being. We'll explore how positive leadership shapes modern organizations, turning challenges into opportunities for growth and transformation. This light side of leadership represents an aspirational and achievable model that resonates deeply in today's dynamic and often uncertain business environment.

The aim of this book is to guide readers through the leadership labyrinth, offering insights and practical tools for navigating the complex spectrum of leadership styles. From the dark side of destructive leadership, through the balanced approach of Militant Neutrality, to the bright realm of positive leadership, this journey provides a comprehensive understanding of leadership dynamics. The book is designed to equip readers with the knowledge and skills necessary to transform their leadership approach and foster more effective, empathetic, and positive leadership in modern organizations.

As you embark on this journey through "From Shadows to Sunshine: Navigating the Leadership Labyrinth," I invite you to reflect on your own experiences and perceptions of leadership. Think about the leaders you've encountered and the styles they embodied. Consider the effects these leaders had on their environments and on you. This reflection is not just an exercise in understanding but also a personal exploration of how you can grow and evolve as a leader. Each chapter will offer opportunities for self-reflection, helping you to apply the insights and strategies in your own life and career.

As we stand at the entrance to the leadership labyrinth, remember that the journey ahead is as challenging as it is rewarding. Will you dare to confront the shadows, balance the scales of neutrality, and embrace the light of positive leadership? This book is your compass and guide through the maze. The path you choose and the leader you become are in your hands. Let's step into the labyrinth together and discover the leader that lies within you.

Part I: "Darth Vader in a Suit: The Dark Side of Leadership"

"The weak are expendable; the strong rise to power."

"In chaos, I find opportunity."

"Power is my ally, and I wield it without restraint."

- Various Sith Lords -

In "Darth Vader in a Suit: The Dark Side of Leadership," the exploration begins by probing the psychological underpinnings that allure certain leaders to dark practices. We delve into the realms of power, control, and fear, peeling back layers to reveal how personality traits like narcissism and Machiavellianism craft a leader's descent into destructive behaviors. The narrative then transitions to the phenomenon of "Toxicity Inc," where the pressures of high stakes, intense competition, and the erosion of ethical boundaries transform potentially good leaders into toxic ones.

As we journey deeper, the narrative unfolds the chilling "Tales from the Dark Side." Here, real-world examples of notorious leaders serve as cautionary tales. These stories bring to life the diverse manifestations of destructive leadership and the profound impacts on organizations and individuals. This section paints a vivid picture of the consequences of such leadership styles, providing a stark reminder of the damages they inflict. Part 1 culminates with "Escape from the Underworld: Overthrowing Darth Vader," offering a beacon of hope. It presents practical strategies and insights on identifying and counteracting the influences of destructive leaders. This part of the narrative focuses on building resilience, promoting ethical behavior, and nurturing a supportive culture. It's about empowering individuals and organizations to rise above the challenges posed by destructive leadership and to foster a healthier, more sustainable leadership environment.

Chapter 1: "Why Some Leaders Love the Dark Side"

As we turn the pages to the first chapter of our exploration into the realms of leadership, we find ourselves venturing into a territory often shrouded in mystery and, sometimes, apprehension: the Dark Side of Leadership. This introductory segment serves as our initial foray into understanding the characteristics that define dark leadership, a concept that, while unsettling, is crucial to comprehend in the broad spectrum of leadership styles.

Here, in the corridors of power and influence, we encounter a paradox. Leadership, traditionally viewed as a vessel for guidance, inspiration, and positive change, can sometimes veer off into a shadowy path. This darker route is lined with traits such as authoritarianism, manipulation, and a notable absence of empathy. Why do some leaders, endowed with the capacity to uplift and empower, choose instead to dominate and control? What magnetic pull does this dark side hold that lures them away from the light of benevolent leadership? In this chapter, we delve deep into these questions, unearthing the roots that feed into the dark side of leadership.

Through a blend of psychological insights, historical examples, and contemporary case studies, we aim to decode the enigma of these dark traits. This exploration is not just an academic exercise; it's a critical journey towards understanding how such leadership styles impact organizations, societies, and the very fabric of our collective human experience. As we embark on this journey, let us brace ourselves to confront some uncomfortable truths, to challenge our preconceptions, and to gain a deeper, more nuanced understanding of what it means to lead—and sometimes, to be led astray.

Dark leadership is often marked by authoritarianism, where the leader exercises strict control over decisions, demanding unquestioned obedience from their team. This style is also rife with manipulation, using cunning or deceit to influence others for the leader's personal gain. A lack of empathy is another key trait, showing a disregard for the feelings, needs, or well-being of others, leading to harsh decisions. Narcissism often surfaces in dark leadership, where an excessive self-focus and egotism are coupled with a disregard for others' perspectives. Machiavellianism is also prevalent, characterized by a cynical disposition to deceive and manipulate for personal gain. Dark leaders tend to exhibit exploitative tendencies, taking advantage of others without concern for their well-being. Their moral flexibility allows them to bend rules or ethical norms to serve personal or organizational ends, and they often use fear as a tool to maintain control and compliance among team members.

Understanding these characteristics of dark leadership is critical for several reasons. It enables prevention and mitigation strategies within organizations and individuals. Recognizing these traits helps foster a healthy organizational culture by contrasting dark leadership with more positive styles. For employees and team members, awareness of these characteristics fosters resilience and informs coping strategies in such environments. Aspiring leaders can use this knowledge for self-reflection, avoiding the pitfalls of dark leadership tendencies. Lastly, this exploration underscores the importance of ethics and morality in leadership, which is essential for sustainable and responsible business practices.

"Power tends to corrupt, and absolute power corrupts absolutely." This famous statement was made by Lord Acton, a British historian of the late nineteenth and early twentieth centuries. In the exploration of dark leadership, one of the most compelling aspects is the lure of power and control. Power, when wielded without checks and balances, has a notorious tendency to corrupt. This corruption is not merely a decline in ethical standards, but a transformation in the leader's perspective and actions. The saying 'power corrupts, and absolute power corrupts absolutely' captures this transformation poignantly. It's a process

where the leader's initial intentions, possibly noble, warp under the weight and seduction of unchecked authority.

The psychological allure of control over others plays a significant role in dark leadership. The ability to influence, direct, and even manipulate people and outcomes can be intoxicating. It feeds into a leader's ego and sense of self-importance, creating a cycle where the more control they exert, the more they desire. This desire for control often stems from deeper psychological needs such as insecurity, a need for dominance, or a response to past experiences where the individual felt powerless.

The complexity of this dynamic is crucial to understand because it's not just the presence of power that leads to dark leadership; it's the relationship the leader has with that power. When power becomes an end in itself, rather than a means to achieve positive outcomes, it sets the stage for the emergence of dark leadership traits. The leader becomes more focused on maintaining and expanding their power and control, often at the expense of ethical considerations, empathy, and the well-being of their team and organization.

Understanding this lure of power and control is essential in recognizing and mitigating the potential for dark leadership. It highlights the need for checks and balances in leadership roles and the importance of self-awareness and ethical grounding for those in positions of power. This insight into the psychological underpinnings of dark leadership is a crucial step in guarding against the drift towards authoritarian and manipulative leadership styles.

The journey into understanding dark leadership necessitates a closer look at specific personality traits that often predispose individuals to such leadership styles. Among these, narcissism, Machiavellianism, and psychopathy stand out as key characteristics frequently associated with dark leadership.

Narcissism in leadership is characterized by an inflated sense of self-importance, a deep need for admiration, and a lack of empathy for others. Narcissistic leaders often see themselves as superior and are preoccupied with fantasies of unlimited success, power, or brilliance. While a certain degree of confidence is necessary for effective leadership, the extreme self-centeredness and grandiosity of narcissism can lead to exploitation of others, ethical lapses, and decision-making that serves the leader's interests at the expense of the organization.

Machiavellianism in leadership refers to a manipulative, cunning, and deceitful approach. Leaders with high levels of Machiavellianism are often skilled in using others as tools to achieve their own goals. They tend to be pragmatic, emotionally detached, and believe that the ends justify the means, regardless of the ethical implications. This trait can lead to a toxic organizational culture, where trust is eroded, and long-term success is sacrificed for short-term gains.

Psychopathy in the context of leadership involves a lack of remorse or guilt, shallow affect, and a failure to accept responsibility for one's actions. Psychopathic leaders may be charismatic and charming, which can be misleading and allow them to rise to high positions of power. However, their lack of empathy, coupled with impulsivity and thrill-seeking behaviors, can result in reckless decision-making and a disregard for the welfare of employees and the organization.

The exploration of these traits is critical in understanding dark leadership, as they provide insight into why certain individuals exhibit destructive and unethical behaviors in leadership roles. Recognizing these traits can help in identifying potentially harmful leaders and in developing strategies to mitigate their negative impact on organizations. Moreover, this understanding emphasizes the importance of comprehensive leadership development programs that not only foster skills and knowledge but also focus on ethical conduct and emotional intelligence.

Real-life examples of leaders who have exhibited traits of narcissism, Machiavellianism, and psychopathy can be drawn from various fields, including business, politics, and other areas.

It's important to note that these examples are based on public perceptions and reported behaviors.

Narcissism: Elizabeth Holmes of Theranos

Elizabeth Holmes, founder and CEO of Theranos, a now-defunct health technology company, was widely reported in the media as exhibiting narcissistic traits. Holmes was known for her ambitious vision to revolutionize blood testing and was initially celebrated for her innovation. However, investigations later revealed that the technology was not as effective as claimed. Reports suggested that her desire for fame and success might have led her to misrepresent her company's capabilities.

Machiavellianism: Richard Nixon, U.S. President

Richard Nixon, the 37th President of the United States, is often cited as an example of Machiavellianism in politics. Nixon's presidency was marked by significant achievements, but also by the Watergate scandal. His involvement in the Watergate cover-up, which was seen as a manipulative and deceitful attempt to protect his administration, ultimately led to his resignation.

Psychopathy: Bernie Madoff, Investment Advisor

Bernie Madoff, an investment advisor, and financier, perpetrated one of the largest Ponzi schemes in history, defrauding investors of billions of dollars. His ability to charm investors, coupled with a lack of remorse for his actions, has been widely discussed in the context of psychopathic traits. Madoff's scheme caused significant financial harm to thousands of people and organizations.

These cases illustrate how the presence of dark leadership traits can lead to significant ethical lapses and have profound consequences. They underscore the importance of ethical leadership and the need for systems and structures that can identify and mitigate the impact of such leadership styles.

The role of organizational culture in nurturing dark leadership is a critical aspect to consider in the context of business ethics and leadership development. Organizational culture can either inhibit or facilitate the emergence and sustainability of dark leadership traits like narcissism, Machiavellianism, and psychopathy. Here's an exploration of how organizational culture can play a role in this dynamic:

1. Cultivation of Power Dynamics: In organizations where power is highly centralized and unquestioned, leaders with dark traits may thrive. A culture that values authority and hierarchy over collaboration and openness can create an environment conducive to authoritarian and manipulative leadership styles.

2. Reward Systems and Incentives: Organizations that reward short-term results and aggressive tactics without considering ethical implications can inadvertently encourage dark leadership traits. When success is measured solely by outcomes like profit or market share, regardless of the methods used to achieve them, leaders may be incentivized to adopt Machiavellian or even psychopathic behaviors to reach these goals.

3. Lack of Accountability and Transparency: In environments where there is little transparency or accountability, leaders with dark traits may operate with impunity. A lack of checks and balances, combined with a culture that doesn't question leadership decisions, can allow unethical behaviors to go unchecked and even become normalized.

4. Toxic Work Environments: Organizational cultures that tolerate or ignore toxic behaviors, such as bullying, harassment, or intimidation, can be breeding grounds for dark leadership. In such environments, empathy and ethical considerations are often devalued, paving the way for narcissistic and psychopathic leaders to rise and dominate.

5. Resistance to Change and Dissent: Cultures that discourage dissent or new ideas can empower dark leaders. When

conformity is prized over critical thinking, and employees fear speaking out against unethical practices, leaders with dark traits can exert control without facing opposition.

6. Admiration of Charismatic Leaders: Organizations that equate charisma with leadership ability may overlook the potential negative aspects of charismatic leaders who may exhibit narcissistic or psychopathic traits. The allure of a charismatic leader can sometimes blind stakeholders to underlying unethical or manipulative behaviors.

7. Failure in Ethical Leadership Development: If an organization lacks a focus on developing ethical leadership and emotional intelligence, it may unintentionally pave the way for leaders with dark traits to emerge. Effective leadership development programs need to emphasize not only skills and competencies but also ethical decision-making and emotional awareness.

Organizational culture plays a pivotal role in either curbing or nurturing dark leadership traits. Cultures that prioritize ethical practices, transparency, accountability, and emotional intelligence are less likely to foster leaders with harmful traits. Conversely, environments that prioritize results over methods, centralize power, and suppress dissent are more likely to see the emergence and success of dark leadership. Understanding this relationship is crucial for organizations aiming to promote ethical leadership and healthy workplace dynamics.

In exploring how certain environments enable or even encourage destructive leadership, it's important to consider various aspects distinct from cultural factors. These environmental elements, though sometimes interwoven with cultural issues, have their own unique impacts on leadership dynamics. Consider the structural frameworks within organizations. Hierarchical and rigid power structures are a significant environmental factor. In such settings, power is concentrated at the top, often leading to a lack of open communication and dissent. This concentration of power can enable leaders to exercise control without checks and balances, fostering an atmosphere where destructive leadership can thrive.

There are high-pressure situations, common in certain industries or organizations facing constant crises or extreme performance pressures. These environments can inadvertently promote a destructive leadership style. Leaders may feel justified in adopting authoritarian or coercive tactics under the guise of urgency, prioritizing immediate results over ethical considerations or team well-being. Another environmental aspect relates to the systems of reward and recognition in place. In organizations where success is measured and rewarded solely based on outcomes like profits or market share, without regard to how these results are achieved, there's a risk of endorsing unethical behavior. This focus on the ends rather than the means can create an environment where destructive leadership is not just tolerated but potentially rewarded.

The issue of accountability plays a crucial role. In environments where there's a lack of robust mechanisms for accountability, destructive leaders can operate with a sense of impunity. Without effective oversight or consequences for unethical behavior, such leaders may feel emboldened to engage in manipulative or abusive practices. Resistance to change is a significant environmental factor. In organizations where innovation and new ideas are met with resistance, leaders who feel threatened by change might suppress these forces. This resistance can lead to a stagnation, where destructive leadership styles are maintained to uphold the status quo, hindering organizational growth and adaptation. The development of emotional intelligence is often overlooked in leadership training within certain environments. When organizations do not prioritize the growth of emotional intelligence among their leaders, they might inadvertently enable destructive leadership. Leaders lacking in self-awareness, empathy, and emotional regulation can unwittingly create negative team dynamics and unhealthy workplace environments.

While there's some overlap with cultural factors, these environmental aspects - structural frameworks, high-pressure situations, reward systems, accountability mechanisms, resistance to change, and emotional intelligence development - play distinct roles in enabling or encouraging destructive leadership.

Addressing these environmental factors is key to fostering healthier and more effective leadership styles.

Analyzing real-life organizations that have fostered destructive leaders can provide valuable insights into how certain environments enable such leadership styles. While specific organizational names are often sensitive and can be subject to legal and ethical considerations, we can discuss generalized scenarios based on well-known cases in the public domain.

Technology Startups with Charismatic Founders

There have been instances in the tech industry where startup founders, often highly charismatic and visionary, have created cultures that inadvertently fostered destructive leadership. These environments, driven by a single leader's vision and personality, sometimes lack the checks and balances typical in more established companies. In such cases, the founder's unchecked power and influence can lead to a culture of fear, a lack of transparency, and unethical decision-making.

Large Financial Institutions Pre-2008 Financial Crisis

Prior to the 2008 financial crisis, certain large financial institutions had cultures that rewarded excessive risk-taking and short-term gains over long-term stability and ethical considerations. In these environments, leaders who engaged in high-risk financial practices were often celebrated and rewarded, leading to a widespread neglect of ethical standards and contributing to the global financial crisis.

Automotive Companies and Safety Scandals

There have been instances in the automotive industry where companies, driven by the pressure to cut costs and maximize profits, overlooked critical safety concerns. In such environments, leaders who prioritized cost-cutting over safety led their organizations into reputational and financial crises due to massive safety recalls and legal issues.

Retail Giants and Labor Practices

Some large retail chains have been criticized for their labor practices, where the pursuit of low prices and high efficiency led to poor working conditions and unethical labor practices. In these companies, leadership that focused solely on financial performance created environments where unethical treatment of workers was overlooked or even tacitly endorsed.

Entertainment and Media Powerhouses

The entertainment and media industry has seen cases where powerful individuals abused their positions, leading to cultures of harassment and exploitation. These environments, often centered around influential figures, lacked sufficient mechanisms to hold leaders accountable, enabling destructive behavior to persist.

These scenarios highlight how certain organizational environments can foster destructive leadership. The common threads in these cases include a lack of accountability, cultures that prioritize financial success over ethics, centralized power structures, and insufficient checks and balances. Understanding these patterns can help organizations in developing strategies to prevent such leadership styles and foster healthier, more ethical, and sustainable organizational cultures.

The phenomenon of dark leadership, while often viewed negatively, can provide a range of psychological and social rewards that appeal to those who adopt this style. One of the most significant draws is the sense of power and control it affords. Leaders exhibiting authoritarian or Machiavellian traits often feel a sense of dominance and superiority, which can be particularly appealing for individuals with a strong desire for control or who have felt powerless in the past. Additionally, narcissistic leaders find dark leadership appealing for the admiration and attention it brings. Leadership positions offer a platform for such individuals to be the center of attention and receive the validation they crave, fueling their self-esteem and ego.

Financial and material gains also play a crucial role. Leaders who engage in unethical practices or prioritize personal gain often reap substantial financial rewards, including high salaries and bonuses. This can be a strong motivator, particularly in environments where financial success is highly valued. For some, the thrill of risk-taking is a reward in itself. Leaders with psychopathic traits may find excitement in engaging in unethical or risky behaviors, especially when they succeed without repercussions, further reinforcing their actions.

The social status and prestige associated with leadership positions offer another reward. Being in a leadership role can provide a sense of pride and accomplishment, particularly in societies that equate leadership with success and authority. The ability to influence others and make impactful decisions can also be rewarding. Even leaders with dark traits can derive satisfaction from shaping the direction of an organization or influencing the behavior and beliefs of their team.

Dark leadership can serve as a means to avoid vulnerability. Adopting a tough, controlling demeanor can shield individuals from criticism or personal and professional challenges. Success through manipulation or deceit can validate the worldview of some leaders, particularly those with Machiavellian traits. This validation is psychologically rewarding, aligning with their beliefs about how the world operates.

The appeal of dark leadership lies in a complex mix of power, admiration, financial incentives, thrill-seeking, social status, influence, protection from vulnerability, and validation of personal worldviews. These factors can drive individuals to engage in dark leadership behaviors, underscoring the need for a comprehensive understanding and approach to addressing and mitigating its impacts.

The allure of dark leadership often lies in its potential for short-term benefits, which can be particularly enticing for leaders predisposed to such styles. These benefits, while they may provide immediate gratification or success, can have long-term negative consequences. However, in the short term, they present a compelling case for leaders inclined towards darker methods.

One of the primary short-term benefits is the rapid accumulation of power and control. Dark leadership styles such as authoritarianism or Machiavellianism can enable leaders to quickly consolidate power and assert control over their organizations. This can be particularly appealing in environments that are highly competitive or in situations where quick decision-making is prized. The immediate results that often accompany dark leadership styles can also be a significant draw. Leaders who employ unethical tactics or who prioritize their own agendas often see quick successes, whether in terms of financial gains, increased market share, or other measurable outcomes. These results can provide a sense of accomplishment and validation for the leader.

Financial rewards are another immediate benefit that can allure leaders to dark leadership. In many cases, the aggressive and ruthless tactics associated with such leadership styles can lead to significant personal financial gains, such as bonuses, higher salaries, or stock options. The sense of autonomy and lack of accountability can also be attractive in the short term. Dark leadership styles often involve making unilateral decisions without needing to consult with or consider the perspectives of others. This can create a sense of freedom and autonomy for the leader, as they feel unencumbered by the need for consensus or collaboration.

The ability to implement one's vision without opposition is a potent allure. Leaders with dark traits may enjoy the ability to execute their plans and strategies without having to justify or explain them to others. This can lead to a sense of efficiency and effectiveness in the short term. The psychological rewards such as the thrill of risk-taking, the sense of superiority, and the validation of personal beliefs can be powerful motivators. These psychological benefits provide a sense of personal satisfaction and achievement, even if they are achieved through unethical or harmful means.

The short-term benefits and allure of dark leadership for the leader include rapid accumulation of power, immediate results, financial rewards, autonomy, the unchallenged implementation of vision, and psychological gratification. However, it's crucial to recognize that these short-term gains often come at a significant long-term cost, both to the leader and the organization.

Leaders may persist in dark leadership behaviors despite negative outcomes for several reasons. These reasons often intertwine with the psychological makeup of the leader, the immediate rewards they receive, and the context or environment in which they operate.

Firstly, the psychological rewards such as a sense of power, control, and admiration can be highly addictive. For leaders exhibiting traits of narcissism, Machiavellianism, or psychopathy, the immediate gratification and affirmation they receive from exerting control or manipulating situations can overshadow the negative long-term consequences. This can create a feedback loop where the leader becomes increasingly reliant on these behaviors to achieve a sense of success or validation.

Secondly, the immediate financial and material gains associated with dark leadership behaviors can be a powerful motivator. In the short term, these behaviors might lead to increased profits, bonuses, or other personal benefits, making it challenging for the leader to abandon these tactics in favor of more ethical and sustainable practices.

Another reason is the lack of immediate or apparent consequences. In some cases, the negative outcomes of dark leadership may not be immediately visible or may be obscured by short-term successes. This can lead the leader to falsely believe that their approach is effective and justified, blinding them to the long-term damage they are causing.

Leaders might also persist in these behaviors due to a lack of awareness or denial. They may not fully recognize the negative impact of their actions on others or the organization. In some cases, they might rationalize their behavior as necessary for the greater good or view any opposition or criticism as unjustified or born of envy.

The environment or culture of the organization can play a significant role. If the organizational culture rewards results over methods, lacks accountability, or is resistant to change, it can encourage the continuation of dark leadership behaviors. In such environments, these behaviors are not only tolerated but sometimes inadvertently encouraged. The fear of vulnerability or change can cause leaders to cling to these behaviors. Admitting the need for change or recognizing the harm caused by their actions requires a level of self-awareness and vulnerability that some leaders might find uncomfortable or threatening. As a result, they continue with the familiar patterns of behavior, even in the face of negative outcomes.

Leaders may persist in dark leadership behaviors due to the addictive nature of the psychological rewards, immediate financial gains, delayed or obscured consequences, lack of self-awareness, enabling organizational environments, and fear of vulnerability or change. These factors create a complex web that can make it challenging for leaders to break out of these destructive patterns, emphasizing the need for robust organizational structures and cultures that promote ethical leadership and accountability.

Let's revisit what some call the Dark Triad in leadership, comprising narcissism, Machiavellianism, and psychopathy, representing a constellation of personality traits that can have profound implications in the corporate world. Each component of the Dark Triad brings its unique set of characteristics, challenges, and impacts when manifested in leadership.

Narcissism in Corporate Leadership

Narcissistic leaders are typically characterized by grandiosity, a need for admiration, and a lack of empathy. They often have a sense of entitlement and an exaggerated sense of self-importance.

In the corporate world, such leaders can initially be charismatic and visionary, attracting followers with their confidence and bold plans. However, their self-centered approach can lead to poor decision-making, as they may ignore valuable feedback and prioritize their interests over the company's. Narcissistic leaders may struggle with criticism and may create a culture of sycophancy, where dissenting voices are silenced, leading to a lack of diverse perspectives and potential blind spots in strategic decision-making.

Machiavellianism in Corporate Leadership

Machiavellian leaders are cunning, manipulative, and often unscrupulous in their pursuit of power. They are adept at deception and are willing to exploit others for their gain. In a business setting, Machiavellian leaders can be effective in navigating corporate politics and may achieve short-term goals through their strategic manipulations. However, this approach can erode trust and cooperation within teams, undermining the long-term health of the organization. Creating a sustainable and ethical corporate culture is difficult with Machiavellian leadership, as such leaders often prioritize their ambitions over ethical considerations and the well-being of their employees.

Psychopathy in Corporate Leadership

Psychopathic leaders display traits like a lack of remorse or guilt, superficial charm, and a shallow emotional experience. They tend to be impulsive and irresponsible. In the corporate context, such leaders can be risk-takers and may initially appear bold and innovative. However, their impulsivity and lack of empathy can lead to reckless decisions and unethical practices, potentially putting the company at risk. Managing the fallout from the actions of a psychopathic leader can be challenging, as they can cause significant harm to a company's reputation and stakeholder relationships. Their lack of concern for rules and social norms can lead to legal and ethical violations.

The presence of Dark Triad traits in leadership can have serious ramifications for a corporation. While some aspects of these traits can be beneficial in specific contexts (such as confidence, strategic thinking, and risk-taking), their negative impacts often outweigh the positives. The challenge for organizations is to recognize these traits and mitigate their harmful effects. This includes implementing strong governance structures, fostering a culture of ethical behavior, and encouraging diverse and open communication to counterbalance the potential destructive tendencies of Dark Triad leaders. Understanding the nuances of these traits helps in developing more balanced and effective leadership within organizations.

Real-life examples of leaders who have exhibited traits associated with the Dark Triad – narcissism, Machiavellianism, and psychopathy – provide insight into the impacts these traits can have in the corporate world. It's important to remember that these are complex psychological constructs, and their manifestation can vary greatly. Here are some generalized examples based on well-documented cases:

Narcissism: High-Profile Tech CEOs

Many leaders in the tech industry have been characterized by their charismatic, visionary, yet highly narcissistic leadership styles. These individuals often attract a great deal of media attention and can initially drive significant innovation and growth in their companies. However, the downsides include making risky, ego-driven business decisions, ignoring critical feedback, and creating a culture where dissent is not tolerated, leading to significant operational and ethical challenges.

Machiavellianism: Corporate Espionage Scandals

Cases of corporate espionage and aggressive competitive tactics in industries like technology and manufacturing often reveal Machiavellian traits in leadership. Leaders in these scenarios have been known to manipulate competitors, employees, and markets to gain an advantage, often leading to legal issues, damaged reputations, and a toxic internal culture that prioritizes winning over ethical behavior.

Psychopathy: Financial Industry Scandals

The financial sector has seen its share of leaders exhibiting psychopathic traits, particularly in cases of fraud and financial misconduct. Such leaders often charm investors and employees alike but lack empathy and remorse, leading to decisions that prioritize personal gain over ethical considerations or the well-being of stakeholders. The consequences have included massive financial losses, legal penalties, and widespread damage to employee morale and public trust.

In each of these cases, the impacts on the organizations and their stakeholders have been significant. While certain traits associated with the Dark Triad can contribute to short-term successes and personal gains for the leaders, the long-term effects are often detrimental. These include damaged organizational reputations, legal and financial repercussions, eroded employee trust and morale, and in some cases, the complete downfall of the company.

These examples underscore the importance of ethical leadership and the need for checks and balances in corporate governance. They highlight the necessity of fostering a corporate culture that values ethical behavior, open communication, and diversity of thought, as a counterbalance to the potential negative impacts of Dark Triad traits in leadership. Identifying early warning signs of a leader turning to the dark side is a crucial aspect of maintaining a healthy organizational culture. These red flags can often be subtle initially but may escalate if unchecked. Recognizing these signs involves being attentive to changes in behavior and attitude that deviate from constructive leadership practices.

A significant warning sign is increasing authoritarianism. This is observed when a leader starts insisting on making all decisions unilaterally, becoming intolerant of input from others, and showing a disregard for democratic processes. Alongside this, growing isolation is another red flag. Leaders who begin to distance themselves from their teams, either physically or by becoming less communicative, might be indicating a shift towards a more self-centered leadership style.

Changes in the way a leader communicates can also be telling. A shift towards manipulative communication, including using deceptive language, withholding information, or playing team members against each other, is concerning. Equally alarming is a noticeable decrease in empathy. This can manifest as insensitivity to others' needs, harsh responses to mistakes, or a general lack of concern for team members' well-being.

An erosion of ethical standards is a critical warning sign. When leaders start bending or breaking rules for personal or organizational gain or begin to justify unethical behavior as a means to an end, it suggests a worrying shift in their moral compass. Similarly, an increasing focus on personal image, reputation, or achievements, often at the expense of the organization's goals or values, indicates a potential turn towards narcissistic leadership.

Rising aggression or intimidation tactics are serious red flags. The use of aggression, intimidation, or fear as tools for compliance or control, such as verbal outbursts or threatening behavior, is indicative of a leader moving towards a more autocratic and potentially destructive style. Resistance to feedback or criticism, especially when met with hostility or defensiveness, also suggests a concerning shift. Finally, an obsession with power and control, including power plays, political maneuvering within the organization, or a fixation on outdoing competitors at any cost, are early indicators of a leader veering towards the dark side.

Recognizing these warning signs is essential for organizations to address potentially harmful shifts in leadership behavior proactively. This can involve offering support, coaching, or training to the concerned leader, fostering a culture of open communication and ethical behavior, and ensuring robust governance and accountability mechanisms are in place.

The seductive nature of the dark side in leadership is a complex and intriguing phenomenon, rooted in the psychological allure and perceived immediate benefits it offers to leaders. This allure often lies in the power, control, and personal gains that come with darker leadership styles, making them an enticing option for some individuals in positions of authority. One of the most compelling aspects of the dark side is the sense of power and control it grants. Leaders who exhibit traits like authoritarianism or Machiavellianism often experience a heightened sense of dominance. This can be particularly appealing to individuals who have a strong desire for control or who have felt powerless in the past. The immediate ability to make unilateral decisions and see direct results of their actions can be intoxicating.

The dark side also offers a shortcut to personal success and recognition. Leaders may be drawn to the rapid accumulation of power and the ability to achieve quick, though often short-lived, successes. This can include financial gains, such as bonuses and high salaries, and the prestige and status that come with successful leadership. For those who equate success with personal gain and power, the dark side presents a seemingly effective path. Additionally, the dark side of leadership can provide a psychological reward. The thrill of risk-taking, the challenge of outmaneuvering opponents, and the validation of personal beliefs and strategies can be highly satisfying. These psychological rewards can reinforce the leader's behavior, creating a feedback loop that encourages the continuation of such practices.

Another seductive aspect is the ability to implement one's vision without opposition. Leaders with dark traits may enjoy executing their plans without needing to justify or explain them to others. This can lead to a sense of efficiency and effectiveness, at least in the short term. However, it's crucial to recognize that the allure of the dark side is often a facade, masking the long-term negative consequences not only for the organization but also for the leader themselves. The initial gains and satisfaction can quickly be overshadowed by the erosion of trust, damaged relationships, and the ultimate decline in organizational health and performance.

The seductive nature of the dark side in leadership is driven by the immediate sense of power, control, personal success, psychological rewards, and the unchallenged implementation of vision it offers. Understanding this allure is essential in developing strategies to prevent leaders from succumbing to these destructive tendencies, emphasizing the importance of ethical leadership and robust organizational cultures.

Dark leadership, with its intricate web of complexities and inherent dangers, presents a significant challenge in the realm of organizational management and personal conduct. At its core, dark leadership encompasses traits and behaviors that, while potentially offering short-term gains, often lead to long-term negative consequences for both leaders and their organizations. One of the primary complexities of dark leadership lies in its seductive nature. The immediate sense of power, control, and personal success that leaders might experience can be misleading. Traits such as authoritarianism, Machiavellianism, and narcissism, often associated with this style, can initially appear effective, especially in environments that prioritize rapid results and strong, decisive leadership. However, this effectiveness is frequently short-lived.

The dangers of dark leadership are manifold. In the pursuit of personal goals and power, dark leaders often neglect or exploit the needs and well-being of their employees, leading to a toxic work environment characterized by fear, low morale, and high turnover. The lack of empathy, ethical considerations, and genuine team engagement can stifle innovation and creativity, ultimately hindering long-term organizational success. Moreover, dark leadership can severely damage an organization's reputation. Unethical decisions and manipulative tactics, once exposed, can lead to a loss of trust among stakeholders, legal ramifications, and a tarnished public image. For the leaders themselves, while the initial ascent might be rapid, the fall can be equally swift and far more damaging, often resulting in career derailments and personal crises. Another complexity arises from the challenge of addressing dark leadership within organizations. Identifying and mitigating these behaviors can be difficult, especially when a leader has entrenched power or when their tactics are subtly woven into their management style. Preventative measures and interventions require a concerted effort, not just at the individual level but also in terms of shaping organizational culture and governance.

The complexities and dangers of dark leadership underscore the need for vigilant and ethical leadership practices. Organizations must foster cultures that value transparency, empathy, and ethical behavior to mitigate the risks associated with dark leadership. Understanding the allure and impact of these leadership styles is crucial for developing effective strategies to prevent and address them, ensuring the long-term health and success of both individuals and their organizations.

Preventing the emergence of dark leadership traits or intervening when they are identified is crucial for maintaining a healthy organizational culture and ensuring effective, ethical leadership. Here are some strategies and interventions that can be employed:

1. Fostering an Ethical Organizational Culture

Emphasize Values: Establish and reinforce a strong set of ethical values that guide behavior and decision-making within the organization.

Lead by Example: Senior leaders and executives should model the ethical behavior they expect from others, demonstrating integrity, transparency, and fairness.

2. Implementing Robust Governance Structures

Clear Policies and Procedures: Have clear policies and procedures that outline acceptable behaviors and practices and ensure these are communicated and understood at all levels.

Accountability Mechanisms: Establish mechanisms for accountability, such as regular audits, performance reviews that include ethical considerations, and channels for reporting unethical behavior.

3. Encouraging Open Communication and Feedback

Feedback Channels: Create safe and confidential channels for employees to provide feedback or report concerns about leadership behavior.

Regular Check-Ins: Encourage regular check-ins and open discussions between leaders and their teams to foster a culture of transparency and open communication.

4. Leadership Training and Development

Ethical Leadership Programs: Implement training programs focused on ethical leadership, emotional intelligence, and effective communication.

Continuous Learning: Encourage leaders to engage in continuous learning and development, emphasizing the importance of self-awareness and empathy.

5. Promoting Diversity and Inclusion

Diverse Perspectives: Cultivate a diverse and inclusive workforce that can offer a range of perspectives and is less susceptible to being dominated by a single, potentially destructive, leadership style.

Inclusive Decision-Making: Encourage inclusive decision-making processes that involve input from various team members.

6. Providing Support and Resources

Counseling and Support Services: Offer access to counseling and support services for leaders and employees to address personal challenges that may impact their leadership style.

Mentorship and Coaching: Provide mentorship and coaching opportunities for leaders to help them develop more balanced and effective leadership skills.

7. Monitoring and Early Intervention

Regular Assessments: Conduct regular assessments of leadership behavior and organizational culture to identify potential issues early.

Intervention Strategies: Have strategies in place for intervening when dark leadership traits are identified, which may include coaching, mentoring, or more direct actions such as reassignment or removal, depending on the severity of the situation.

By implementing these preventative measures and interventions, organizations can create an environment that discourages dark leadership traits and promotes a culture of ethical, effective leadership. This not only benefits the organizational health but also contributes to the overall well-being and satisfaction of all employees.

The importance of awareness and proactive management in leadership roles cannot be overstated. In the dynamic and often complex world of organizational leadership, being aware and proactive is essential for fostering a healthy work environment, achieving sustainable success, and navigating the myriad challenges that come with managing people and resources. Awareness in leadership involves a deep understanding of various aspects: self-awareness, awareness of others, and awareness of the broader organizational context. Self-awareness allows leaders to recognize their strengths and weaknesses, understand their impact on others, and manage their behaviors and decisions more effectively. It is also crucial for identifying personal biases and avoiding decisions that stem from ego or self-interest.

Awareness of others is equally important. This encompasses understanding the needs, motivations, and concerns of team members and colleagues. Such awareness fosters empathy and helps in building strong, trust-based relationships. It enables leaders to communicate effectively, provide meaningful support, and engage their teams in a manner that motivates and inspires. Awareness of the broader organizational context involves understanding the company's culture, values, and goals. It also includes staying informed about industry trends, market dynamics, and other external factors that might affect the organization. This broader awareness is key for strategic planning, risk management, and ensuring that the organization remains relevant and competitive.

Proactive management complements this awareness. Proactive leaders do not just react to situations as they arise but anticipate challenges and opportunities. They plan ahead, set clear goals and strategies, and take decisive action to steer their team and organization towards success. Proactive management involves not only dealing with immediate issues but also preparing for future challenges and actively pursuing growth and development opportunities. In the context of potential negative leadership styles or organizational issues, proactive management is critical. Leaders need to actively cultivate a positive culture, address any signs of toxic behavior, and implement strategies to prevent issues like burnout, conflict, or ethical lapses. This might involve regular training, establishing clear policies and communication channels, and creating an environment where feedback is encouraged and valued.

Awareness and proactive management are vital in leadership roles. They enable leaders to understand themselves, their teams, and their operating environments better, and to act in ways that promote the well-being and success of both their people and their organization. These qualities help in building resilient, adaptable, and ethical leaders who are equipped to handle the complexities of the modern business world.

Chapter 2: "Toxicity Inc: When Leaders Turn Bad"

The journey into understanding how good leaders can turn toxic is both intriguing and crucial for any organization seeking to foster a positive work environment. This chapter explores the transformation process, exploring the various factors and circumstances that can cause a well-intentioned leader to deviate towards a more detrimental leadership style. We begin by acknowledging that not all toxic leaders start off with negative intentions or destructive personality traits. Many begin their leadership journey with the same aspirations as any effective leader – to inspire, to drive success, and to positively impact their organizations and teams. However, along the way, a complex interplay of factors can trigger a shift, leading these once-promising leaders down a path of toxicity.

One of the key aspects we examine is the role of external pressures. This includes the stress of meeting high expectations, the relentless pursuit of targets and goals, and the constant scrutiny that leadership positions entail. These pressures can sometimes cause leaders to adopt a more aggressive, authoritarian style as a means of coping or maintaining control. Another significant factor is the influence of the organizational environment and culture. Leaders do not operate in a vacuum; they are influenced by the values, behaviors, and norms that pervade their workplace. An environment that implicitly rewards cutthroat competitiveness, for instance, might gradually lead a leader to adopt similar traits.

The chapter also delves into the impact of personal challenges and changes. Personal crises, significant life changes, or even the gradual buildup of smaller stresses and pressures can alter a leader's behavior. The way a leader deals with these challenges can significantly impact their leadership style and approach to decision-making. Additionally, we look at the potential for power to alter a leader's perspective and actions. The old adage that "power corrupts" comes into play here again, as we explore how the intoxication of power can sometimes lead to a loss of empathy, increased risk-taking, and a focus on personal gain over the collective good.

In understanding the transformation of good leaders into toxic ones, it is important to recognize that this process is often gradual and not always immediately apparent. By closely examining these and other contributing factors, this chapter sets the stage for a deeper understanding of how toxicity develops in leadership and what can be done to prevent it. This exploration is crucial for anyone looking to nurture positive leadership and mitigate the risks associated with leadership gone awry.

Let's explore the psychological underpinnings of how good leaders can transform into toxic ones. Understanding this transformation is key to preventing and addressing toxic leadership in organizations. The psychological journey from effective to toxic leadership often involves a combination of personal vulnerabilities, cognitive biases, and reactions to environmental stressors. Initially, many leaders start with positive intentions, but various psychological factors can gradually lead them astray.

One critical factor is the response to power and success. Psychological studies have shown that power can have an intoxicating effect, altering a leader's perception and behavior. Leaders might start to overestimate their capabilities, become less empathetic, and more self-centered. This shift can lead to a sense of invulnerability and a tendency to dismiss or undervalue the input of others.

Stress and pressure are also key elements in this transformation. The constant pressure to perform and meet high expectations can take a toll on a leader's mental well-being. In response to stress, some leaders might adopt a more controlling or aggressive style as a defensive mechanism. This can be exacerbated by a lack of adequate support or coping mechanisms.

The concept of cognitive dissonance plays a role too. When leaders' actions do not align with their values or the perceived values of their role, it creates psychological discomfort. To alleviate this discomfort, leaders may either change their actions or change their beliefs to justify their actions. Unfortunately, the latter can lead to a rationalization of toxic behavior. Another psychological aspect is the influence of biases and flawed decision-making. Confirmation bias, for example, can lead leaders to favor information that confirms their preexisting beliefs or decisions, while ignoring contradictory evidence. Over time, this can lead to increasingly poor and harmful decision-making.

The gradual nature of the transformation is a key psychological element. Often, the shift towards toxic behavior is incremental, making it hard for leaders to recognize their behavioral changes. This 'boiling frog' phenomenon means that by the time the leader, or those around them, recognize the toxicity, the patterns are well-established and more difficult to change. The interaction between the leader's personality traits and the organizational environment can catalyze the shift to toxic leadership. For instance, a leader with a tendency towards narcissism may have this trait exacerbated in a highly competitive, achievement-focused environment.

The psychology behind the transformation from a good to a toxic leader is multifaceted, involving a complex interplay of power dynamics, stress and pressure, cognitive dissonance, biases, the gradual nature of behavioral changes, and the interaction between personal traits and the organizational environment. Understanding these psychological aspects is crucial for identifying early warning signs and implementing effective interventions to prevent or address toxic leadership.

What about the significant role that high-pressure environments play in contributing to the development of toxic leadership? High stakes and intense demands are common in many modern workplaces, and understanding how these pressures can catalyze a shift towards toxic leadership is essential for any organization.

High-pressure environments are often characterized by tight deadlines, ambitious targets, intense competition, and high expectations. Leaders in such settings are under constant scrutiny to perform and deliver results. While some degree of pressure can be motivating and lead to high performance, excessive pressure can have the opposite effect.

Under extreme pressure, the fear of failure becomes a dominant force. Leaders may start to perceive every decision as critical and every mistake as catastrophic. This heightened fear can lead to a defensive leadership style, where the leader becomes more controlling, rigid, and less tolerant of perceived weaknesses or dissent. The focus shifts from collaborative success to avoiding failure at all costs. Moreover, high stakes often blur the lines between ethical and unethical behavior. In a bid to meet targets and outperform competitors, leaders may resort to questionable practices. This might include cutting corners, manipulating data, or pushing teams beyond reasonable limits. Over time, this can foster a culture where ends justify the means, eroding ethical standards and normalizing toxic behaviors.

Another aspect of high-pressure environments is the impact on decision-making. Stress can impair cognitive functions, leading to short-sighted or biased decisions. Leaders might rely on heuristics or 'gut feelings' rather than thorough analysis, increasing the risk of flawed judgments. In their haste to resolve immediate pressures, they may overlook long-term consequences, setting the stage for future crises. High-pressure environments can also exacerbate existing vulnerabilities or negative traits in leaders. For instance, a leader with a tendency towards narcissism may become increasingly self-centered under pressure, while one with authoritarian tendencies may become excessively domineering.

Constant high pressure can lead to burnout, a state of emotional, mental, and physical exhaustion. Burnout can significantly alter a leader's behavior, causing them to become detached, cynical, and less effective in their role. This detachment can manifest as a lack of empathy and concern for the well-being of their team, a key characteristic of toxic leadership.

High-pressure environments play a crucial role in the development of toxic leadership. The intense demands and high stakes can lead to fear-driven, unethical, and short-sighted decision-making, exacerbate negative traits, and even cause burnout. Recognizing and managing the pressures faced by leaders is vital in preventing the slide into toxic leadership behaviors. This involves creating a supportive environment, setting realistic targets, encouraging ethical practices, and providing resources for leaders to manage stress effectively.

In exploring different real-life examples of leaders who have succumbed to high-stakes pressures, we find instances across various sectors that illustrate how intense demands can lead to problematic leadership decisions and behaviors.

Healthcare Industry and Cost-Cutting Measures

In the healthcare sector, there have been cases where hospital administrators and healthcare executives, under immense pressure to reduce costs while improving patient care, have made decisions that compromised patient safety. This includes understaffing critical units or reducing spending on essential equipment, leading to lower standards of care and increased patient risks.

Media Industry and Ethical Lapses

High-profile cases in the media industry have shown how leaders, driven by the pressure to increase viewership and revenue, have engaged in unethical practices. This includes prioritizing sensationalism over factual reporting or overlooking inappropriate behavior within their organizations to protect their brand.

Sports Leadership and Performance Pressure

In the world of professional sports, coaches and team managers have sometimes succumbed to the pressure to win at all costs. This has led to instances of pushing athletes beyond safe limits, neglecting their health and well-being, or even condoning the use of performance-enhancing substances.

Educational Institutions and Admission Scandals

Leaders in prestigious educational institutions have been caught in high-profile admission scandals. Under pressure to maintain the reputation and exclusivity of their institutions, some have engaged in fraudulent admissions practices, unfairly favoring certain applicants over more qualified ones.

Non-Profit Organizations and Misallocation of Funds

In the non-profit sector, there have been instances where leaders, faced with the dual pressures of delivering results to beneficiaries and pleasing donors, have misallocated funds or exaggerated program successes, thereby betraying the trust of their supporters and those they serve.

These examples from diverse sectors highlight that no industry is immune to the dangers of high-pressure environments on leadership decision-making. They illustrate the need for strong ethical frameworks, transparent practices, and support systems that help leaders navigate challenging situations without compromising their values or the well-being of those they are responsible for. These cases serve as a reminder of the importance of ethical vigilance and resilience in leadership roles.

Competition, while a natural and often beneficial aspect of the business world, can act as a catalyst for toxic leadership behaviors when it becomes excessively intense or is handled improperly. The drive to outperform rivals, achieve market dominance, or meet aggressive targets can push some leaders to adopt harmful strategies and behaviors. In highly competitive environments, the pressure to succeed often becomes paramount. Leaders may feel that the only way to survive and thrive is to be the best at all costs. This mindset can lead to a win-at-all-costs attitude, where the end goal of outperforming the competition justifies the means, regardless of their ethical implications.

One manifestation of this is the prioritization of results over process. Leaders might become so focused on beating competitors or achieving specific metrics that they neglect how these results are obtained. This can lead to cutting corners, bending rules, and making decisions that, while they may yield short-term gains, are unsustainable or unethical in the long run. Another aspect is the erosion of teamwork and internal collaboration. In an overly competitive environment, leaders may foster a culture of internal competition, where team members are pitted against each other. While healthy internal competition can be motivating, taken to extremes, it can create a toxic work environment characterized by distrust, backstabbing, and a lack of cooperation.

Excessive competition can lead to a heightened fear of failure. Leaders in these environments might perceive any setback or underperformance as catastrophic, leading to overreaction, stress, and decision-making driven by fear rather than rational analysis. This fear can stifle innovation and risk-taking, as leaders become more conservative and risk-averse in their decision-making. In their quest to outdo competitors, leaders might also resort to aggressive or unethical marketing and sales tactics. This includes misleading advertising, overly aggressive sales practices, or denigrating competitors, which can harm the organization's reputation and lead to legal and ethical repercussions. Excessive competition can exacerbate personal vulnerabilities in leaders. For example, a leader with a tendency towards narcissism may become more self-centered and less empathetic, while one with authoritarian tendencies may become more controlling and dictatorial.

Competition, when it escalates into an all-consuming focus, can be a potent catalyst for toxic leadership behaviors. It can distort priorities, undermine ethical standards, and create a damaging work culture. Recognizing and managing the effects of competition is essential for leaders to ensure that their drive to succeed does not lead them or their organizations astray. This involves striking a balance between healthy competition and maintaining ethical, collaborative, and sustainable business practices.

In exploring how competitive environments can precipitate toxic leadership, various industry scenarios come to mind. These hypothetical case studies, though not based on specific real-life events, reflect common patterns observed in sectors where competition is intense.

Consider a scenario in the advertising industry. A once-thriving agency, known for its creative edge, starts losing market share to newer, more dynamic competitors. The pressure to regain top position leads the CEO to adopt a win-at-all-costs mentality. In the race to outperform rivals, the CEO pushes teams to their limits, demanding innovative campaigns with unrealistic deadlines. Morale plummets as creativity is stifled by stress and exhaustion, leading to a talent exodus and a decline in the quality of work. The agency, once celebrated for its vibrant culture and groundbreaking work, becomes known for its high turnover and declining client satisfaction.

In the world of corporate law, a law firm known for its prestigious clientele faces new competitors offering lower rates and aggressive marketing. To maintain its elite status, the firm's leadership imposes stringent billing targets on its attorneys. The pressure to meet these targets leads to overbilling practices and an unhealthy work culture characterized by long hours and ethical compromises. The firm's reputation suffers as clients begin to question the integrity of their legal counsel, leading to a loss of trust and a downturn in business.

The hospitality industry provides another example. A hotel chain, in an effort to outshine its competitors in luxury and service, begins to cut corners on operational costs. The management, driven by the desire to impress stakeholders with short-term financial gains, overlooks the importance of staff training and maintenance. This short-sighted approach leads to a decline in service quality and guest satisfaction. Negative reviews and a tarnished brand image soon follow, undoing the chain's years of reputation building.

These scenarios across different industries illustrate how the pressure to outperform competitors can lead to detrimental leadership decisions. The focus on immediate success and market dominance can cloud judgment, leading to a neglect of the very foundations that ensure long-term success: employee well-being, ethical practices, and sustainable growth strategies. They underscore the importance of ethical leadership and a balanced approach to competition, vital for maintaining a healthy organizational culture and reputation in the long run.

The impact of unrealistic goals and expectations on leaders is profound, affecting not just their leadership style and decision-making but also their personal well-being and the health of the organizations they lead. When leaders are constantly faced with objectives that are unattainable or expectations that are excessively high, it can lead to a range of negative outcomes.

Firstly, unrealistic goals can create immense pressure on leaders. This pressure often results in stress and anxiety, which can impair judgment and decision-making abilities. Leaders might resort to short-term, high-risk strategies or make hasty decisions without fully considering the consequences, prioritizing immediate results over long-term sustainability. This pressure can also lead to burnout, a state of physical, emotional, and mental exhaustion. Burnout not only affects a leader's health and productivity but also their ability to engage and inspire their teams. A leader who is burned out may become detached, less empathetic, and more prone to negative emotions, such as frustration and cynicism.

In an effort to meet unrealistic expectations, leaders might also develop toxic behaviors. This can manifest as authoritarianism, where leaders become overly controlling, or Machiavellianism, where they use manipulation to achieve their goals. Such behaviors can create a toxic work environment, eroding trust, diminishing team morale, and increasing employee turnover.

The focus on unachievable goals can lead to a culture of fear and blame within the organization. Leaders might start to blame their teams for failures or shortcomings, creating an environment where people are afraid to take risks or think creatively. This stifles innovation and can lead to a decline in the overall performance of the organization. The constant pursuit of unrealistic goals can also lead to ethical lapses. In the desperation to deliver results, leaders may overlook ethical considerations, leading to practices that are not only unsustainable but potentially harmful to the organization's reputation and long-term success.

Such an environment can cause a misalignment between the leader's values and actions. Leaders might find themselves compromising on their principles to achieve targets, leading to internal conflict and dissatisfaction. This misalignment can diminish a leader's sense of purpose and fulfillment in their role.

The impact of unrealistic goals and expectations on leaders is multi-faceted, affecting their mental health, leadership style, ethical compass, and the overall health of their organization. It underscores the importance of setting realistic, achievable objectives, providing support for leaders to manage stress, and fostering a culture that values ethical behavior and long-term success over short-term gains.

The link between corporate culture, unrealistic targets, and leader toxicity is a critical issue in organizational dynamics. When a corporate culture is steeped in excessively high expectations and unattainable goals, it can significantly contribute to the development of toxic leadership behaviors. In a corporate culture that emphasizes unrealistic targets, success is often measured by the ability to meet or exceed these high benchmarks. This relentless push for extraordinary performance can create an environment where the ends justify the means. Leaders in such settings may feel immense pressure to deliver results at any cost, leading them to adopt harmful tactics.

This pressure can manifest in various forms of toxic leadership:

1. Authoritarianism: To meet high targets, leaders may become overly controlling, imposing strict rules and expecting blind obedience. They might stifle creativity and innovation,

insisting on proven methods that guarantee results, even if such methods are unsustainable or detrimental in the long term.

2. Manipulation: Leaders might resort to manipulative tactics to achieve desired outcomes. This can include distorting information, overpromising, or setting unrealistic benchmarks for their teams, creating a cycle of stress and disappointment.

3. Neglect of Employee Well-being: In the pursuit of goals, leaders may overlook the well-being of their team members. This neglect can lead to a toxic work environment characterized by burnout, high turnover, and a decrease in overall employee morale and engagement.

4. Ethical Compromises: The drive to hit unrealistic targets can lead leaders to make ethically questionable decisions. This might involve cutting corners, overlooking regulatory requirements, or engaging in unfair practices against competitors or within the organization.

5. Fear-based Leadership: A culture driven by unrealistic goals often instills fear of failure among leaders. This fear can translate into toxic behaviors where leaders use intimidation or punitive measures to drive their teams, leading to a culture of fear within the organization.

6. Erosion of Trust and Team Cohesion: As leaders become more focused on targets and less on people, trust within the team can erode. Team members may feel undervalued and disengaged, leading to poor collaboration and a lack of cohesion.

Corporate cultures that propagate unrealistic targets often fail to recognize the long-term consequences of such an approach. While they may drive short-term gains, they can lead to a host of negative outcomes, including toxic leadership, ethical scandals, high employee turnover, and ultimately, a decline in organizational performance and reputation. Addressing this issue requires a shift in corporate culture to value sustainable growth, ethical behavior, and employee well-being as much as, if not more than, meeting aggressive targets. This involves setting realistic goals, creating supportive environments for leaders and employees, and fostering a culture of open communication and ethical practices. By doing so, organizations can mitigate the risk of leader toxicity and build a more resilient and healthier organizational environment.

The concept of moral disengagement plays a pivotal role in how ethical standards are sometimes sidestepped, allowing leaders to justify actions that might otherwise clash with their moral compass. This slippery slope of moral disengagement is a process where leaders gradually, often unknowingly, begin to rationalize unethical behaviors, leading to a normalization of such actions. Moral disengagement begins with the subtle art of euphemistic labeling, where leaders use sanitized language to describe unethical actions, making them seem less harmful. For instance, downsizing is termed 'right-sizing', lending a less negative connotation to the act. In other instances, leaders engage in advantageous comparison, where they justify their questionable actions by comparing them to more egregious behaviors, making their own seem relatively benign.

A key aspect of moral disengagement is the displacement of responsibility. Leaders attribute their choices to external pressures such as market demands or directives from superiors, thus distancing themselves from the responsibility of their actions. Closely related is the diffusion of responsibility, especially prevalent in organizational settings where decision-making is a collective process. In such environments, the shared nature of decision-making can dilute personal accountability, making it easier for leaders to partake in unethical decisions.

Leaders may engage in the disregard or distortion of consequences. By minimizing the negative outcomes of their actions or convincing themselves that the consequences aren't severe, they reduce the cognitive dissonance between their actions and their ethical standards. Another disturbing facet is dehumanization, where those affected by unethical actions are viewed impersonally. This depersonalization allows leaders to justify their actions without confronting the human cost. Attribution of blame plays a role in moral disengagement. Leaders sometimes blame the victims of their unethical actions, convincing themselves that those affected are somehow at fault and deserving of their fate. This further entrenches the leaders in their unethical path, as they view themselves as blameless.

Understanding the nuances of moral disengagement is crucial in preventing unethical behavior in leadership. It calls for fostering a culture of ethical vigilance, where rationalizations are challenged, open communication is encouraged, and the focus is kept on the human impact of business decisions. By being aware of the slippery slope of moral disengagement, organizations can take proactive steps to ensure their leaders uphold ethical standards, thereby maintaining integrity and trustworthiness in their leadership roles.

The psychological mechanisms behind moral disengagement involve intricate mental processes that enable individuals, including leaders, to rationalize or justify unethical or harmful behavior. These mechanisms work by altering a person's perception of their actions, effectively reducing the moral discomfort associated with violating ethical standards. One key process is the cognitive reconstruction of actions. This involves reframing unethical behaviors in ways that make them appear more acceptable or benign. For example, leaders might use euphemistic language to soften the impact of their decisions, such as describing layoffs as "streamlining the workforce," which obscures the reality of job loss.

Moral justification is another mechanism where leaders convince themselves that their unethical actions serve a higher purpose. By adopting a belief that the ends justify the means, they view their actions as necessary for achieving greater organizational success or competitive advantage.

In group or organizational contexts, the diffusion of responsibility plays a significant role. Responsibility for decisions is often shared among multiple individuals, leading to a situation where no single person feels fully accountable for unethical actions. This can result in leaders feeling less guilty about their involvement because the decision was collective. Closely related is the displacement of responsibility, where leaders attribute their unethical actions to external demands or orders from higher authorities. By claiming they were just following company policies or directives from superiors, leaders can justify their actions and absolve themselves from personal responsibility.

Distortion of consequences involves minimizing or overlooking the harm caused by one's actions. By downplaying the negative impact of their decisions, leaders can reduce the moral weight of their actions, making it easier to proceed without experiencing guilt. Dehumanization of victims is another mechanism where leaders strip away the humanity of those affected by their decisions. By viewing them as mere statistics or objects, rather than people with feelings and rights, it becomes easier to commit acts that harm others, as the emotional and empathetic response is muted. Attribution of blame involves rationalizing that the victims of unethical behavior were at fault or deserved the outcome. This rationalization helps leaders absolve themselves of responsibility and guilt, maintaining their positive self-image.

These psychological mechanisms often operate subconsciously and can be potent forces in driving behavior. They allow leaders to maintain a positive self-image and avoid the discomfort of acknowledging their unethical actions. Recognizing and understanding these mechanisms is crucial in combating moral disengagement. Promoting self-awareness, ethical training, and a culture of accountability are key steps organizations can take to help leaders align with moral and ethical values, especially in challenging situations.

The effects of toxic leadership on organizational culture are profound and far-reaching. When a leader exhibits toxic behaviors, it not only impacts their immediate team but can permeate through the entire organization, affecting morale, productivity, and the overall workplace atmosphere. One of the most immediate effects is the erosion of trust. Toxic leaders often break down the trust that is foundational to effective teamwork and collaboration. Employees may start to feel uncertain about their leader's decisions, motives, and integrity. This distrust can extend to the broader organization, leading to a general atmosphere of skepticism and apprehension.

Toxic leadership also creates a culture of fear and compliance rather than one of engagement and creativity. Employees under a toxic leader may feel that they are constantly walking on eggshells, leading them to avoid taking risks or proposing new ideas. This stifles innovation and can hinder the organization's ability to adapt and grow. This kind of leadership often results in decreased employee morale and job satisfaction. The negative atmosphere created by such leadership can lead to increased stress and burnout among employees. This not only affects their well-being but also their engagement and commitment to the organization. High turnover rates are a common consequence, as employees leave in search of healthier work environments.

Additionally, toxic leadership can lead to poor communication within the organization. Fear of retribution or the belief that their concerns will not be addressed can lead employees to withhold information, avoid discussions, and disengage from meaningful communication. This lack of open communication can result in misunderstandings, missed opportunities, and an inability to effectively address and resolve issues. The impact on the organization's reputation is another significant concern. Stories of toxic leadership and an unhealthy workplace culture can quickly spread beyond the organization, affecting its reputation in the industry. This can make it difficult to attract and retain top talent and can even impact customer perceptions and business relationships.

Finally, toxic leadership can have a lasting impact on the organization's values and norms. Over time, the negative behaviors and attitudes modeled by a toxic leader can become normalized, altering the fundamental character of the organization. Reversing this shift can be a significant challenge and may require comprehensive changes in leadership and organizational culture.

The effects of toxic leadership on organizational culture are detrimental and multifaceted. They manifest in eroded trust, a culture of fear, decreased employee morale, poor communication, a damaged reputation, and an alteration of the organization's core values and norms. Addressing toxic leadership is crucial for the health and success of any organization, requiring a proactive approach to foster a positive and supportive workplace culture.

In the corporate landscape, there are numerous real-life examples where toxic leaders have transformed workplaces for the worse, illustrating the significant impact of leadership on organizational culture.

In the world of publishing, there was a case where a renowned magazine was steered by a charismatic but ultimately toxic editor-in-chief. Under their tenure, the editor's aggressive and demeaning style led to a culture of fear and anxiety among the staff. The once collaborative and innovative atmosphere turned competitive and stifling, leading to a decline in the quality of content and a high turnover rate among the editorial staff. This change negatively affected the magazine's reputation and readership.

In the hospitality industry, a hotel chain experienced a drastic transformation under a new management team. The management's relentless focus on cost-cutting and efficiency, coupled with a disregard for staff welfare, led to widespread discontent. Employee morale plummeted due to unreasonable workloads and a lack of appreciation, which in turn affected customer service standards. The chain, once praised for its customer service, faced a barrage of negative reviews and a decline in guest loyalty.

The manufacturing sector has also seen its share of toxic leadership. A factory known for its worker-friendly policies underwent a drastic change when a new plant manager was appointed. The manager's authoritarian approach, marked by strict rules and little regard for worker safety, led to a significant increase in workplace accidents and a decrease in product quality. The workers' dissatisfaction culminated in strikes and reputational damage for the company, highlighting the cost of neglecting employee welfare.

In the field of academia, a prestigious university department was impacted by the leadership of a new department head. The head's narcissistic leadership style, characterized by favoritism and a dismissive attitude towards faculty concerns, led to internal conflicts and a decline in department morale. This toxic environment not only affected the faculty's productivity and well-being but also impeded the department's ability to attract and retain talented academics and students.

These examples from various industries demonstrate the pervasive and detrimental effects of toxic leadership. They highlight the need for organizations to vigilantly monitor and address leadership behaviors, ensuring that the work environment remains conducive to employee well-being, productivity, and the overall success of the organization.

Organizations aiming to prevent and mitigate toxic leadership can adopt a multi-faceted approach. This approach should focus on fostering a positive organizational culture, implementing robust governance structures, and ensuring ongoing leadership development and accountability. Here's how organizations can strategize against toxic leadership:

1. Cultivating a Positive Organizational Culture

Emphasize Ethical Values: Embed ethical values into the organization's culture. This involves not just stating values but living them through actions and decisions at every level.

Promote Open Communication: Encourage a culture where feedback is welcomed and valued. Ensure that employees at all levels feel safe and comfortable voicing concerns or reporting toxic behavior.

2. Robust Recruitment and Selection Processes

Screen for Leadership Qualities: During recruitment, focus on leadership qualities like empathy, integrity, and teamwork. Behavioral interviews and psychological assessments can be valuable tools.

Thorough Background Checks: Conduct thorough background checks to identify any past instances of problematic behavior.

3. Leadership Development and Training

Regular Training: Implement ongoing training programs focused on ethical leadership, emotional intelligence, and effective communication.

Mentorship and Coaching: Offer mentorship and coaching for leaders to develop their skills and address any areas of concern.

4. Implementing Effective Governance Structures

Clear Policies and Procedures: Develop clear policies and procedures that define acceptable behavior and the consequences of toxicity.

Accountability Mechanisms: Establish strong accountability mechanisms to ensure leaders are held responsible for their actions.

5. Encouraging Work-Life Balance

Promote Balance: Encourage a culture that values work-life balance to reduce stress and burnout, which can contribute to toxic behavior.

6. Regular Performance and Feedback Mechanisms

360-Degree Feedback: Use comprehensive feedback systems, like 360-degree reviews, to assess leadership performance from multiple perspectives.

Performance Metrics: Include behavioral and ethical considerations in performance metrics for leaders.

7. Providing Support Systems:

Access to Counseling: Offer access to counseling or support services for leaders to address stress, burnout, or personal issues that may impact their leadership style.

Employee Assistance Programs: Implement Employee Assistance Programs (EAPs) to provide support for all employees.

8. Swift and Decisive Action Against Toxicity:

Zero Tolerance Policy: Enforce a zero-tolerance policy against toxic behavior, ensuring that any issues are addressed swiftly and decisively.

9. Regular Organizational Reviews:

Culture Audits: Conduct regular organizational culture audits to identify and address any signs of toxicity.

Adaptability and Change: Be open to change and continuously adapt strategies based on feedback and evolving organizational needs.

By implementing these strategies, organizations can create an environment where toxic leadership is less likely to develop or go unchecked. This proactive approach is essential for maintaining a healthy and productive work environment that supports the well-being and success of all employees.

To maintain ethical and healthy leadership practices, leaders can utilize a variety of tools and strategies. These tools are designed to help leaders navigate the complexities of their roles while upholding high ethical standards and fostering a positive work environment.

One effective tool is ongoing training and development focused on ethical leadership and emotional intelligence. Engaging in regular workshops, seminars, and courses helps leaders stay aware of best practices and new developments in ethical leadership. This continuous learning approach keeps leaders informed and adept at handling various situations ethically and effectively. Another vital tool is self-reflection and self-awareness exercises. Regular self-assessment helps leaders understand their strengths and areas for improvement, particularly regarding their impact on others. Tools like journaling, mindfulness practices, and feedback mechanisms allow leaders to reflect on their actions and decisions, ensuring they remain aligned with ethical standards.

Mentorship and coaching provide leaders with guidance and support. Having a mentor or coach who can offer advice, share experiences, and provide an outside perspective is invaluable. This relationship can help leaders navigate challenges, make better decisions, and stay grounded in ethical practices. Establishing a strong support network is also essential. This network can include peers, superiors, or external advisors who can offer different perspectives, advice, and support. A diverse network enables leaders to discuss challenges and solutions in a confidential and supportive environment.

Adopting a participative leadership style is another effective tool. By involving team members in decision-making, leaders can ensure diverse perspectives are considered, enhancing the ethical decision-making process. This inclusive approach also promotes a positive organizational culture and increases team engagement and satisfaction. Utilizing feedback systems, such as 360-degree feedback, allows leaders to receive comprehensive feedback on their performance from superiors, peers, and subordinates. This feedback is crucial for identifying areas of improvement and for understanding the impact of their leadership style on others.

Leaders can also benefit from clear ethical guidelines and decision-making frameworks. Having a set of principles or a framework to guide decisions ensures that actions are consistent with the organization's values and ethical standards. Finally, prioritizing work-life balance and personal well-being is crucial. By taking care of their physical and mental health, leaders are better equipped to handle stress, make clear-headed decisions, and set a positive example for their teams.

Incorporating these tools into their leadership practice, leaders can maintain a healthy, ethical approach to leadership, ensuring their impact on the organization and its people is positive and sustainable.

Recognizing and halting the slide into toxicity is crucial for leaders to maintain a healthy organizational culture and effective leadership. The first step in this process is self-awareness. Leaders need to be vigilant about their behaviors and attitudes, constantly reflecting on their actions and the impact they have on others. This can be achieved through regular self-reflection, seeking feedback, and being open to constructive criticism. It's also important for leaders to understand the stressors and triggers that might lead to toxic behaviors. This understanding can come from self-analysis or through discussions with mentors, coaches, or therapists. By identifying these triggers, leaders can develop strategies to manage stress and avoid reacting in ways that can be harmful to themselves and their teams.

Creating and maintaining a strong support network is another key aspect. This network should include peers, mentors, and other trusted individuals who can provide honest feedback and guidance. Having people to talk to about challenges and concerns can help leaders stay grounded and avoid the isolation that often accompanies toxic leadership.

Leaders should also set clear boundaries and ensure they have a healthy work-life balance. Overwork and stress are significant contributors to toxic behavior, so it's important for leaders to take care of their physical and mental health. This includes regular exercise, hobbies, and spending time with family and friends.

Regular training and development focused on ethical leadership and emotional intelligence can also help leaders stay on the right path. Such training provides leaders with the tools and knowledge to lead in a way that is respectful, empathetic, and ethically sound. Implementing a feedback mechanism within the organization can aid in early detection of toxic tendencies. Encouraging open communication and creating a safe environment for employees to voice concerns can help in identifying and addressing issues before they escalate.

Leaders should practice humility and empathy, constantly reminding themselves of the impact their leadership has on others. They should strive to understand and appreciate the perspectives and needs of their team members, fostering an inclusive and supportive work environment. If toxic behaviors do start to develop, it's essential for leaders to take swift and decisive action to correct their course. This might involve seeking professional help, such as coaching or counseling, or making significant changes in their leadership approach and work environment. By recognizing the early signs of toxicity and taking proactive steps to address them, leaders can prevent the harmful effects of toxic leadership and foster a positive, productive, and ethical organizational culture.

In summarizing the key takeaways from the chapter on recognizing and halting the slide into toxicity, several crucial points emerge:

1. Self-Awareness is Critical: The first step in avoiding toxic leadership is self-awareness. Leaders need to regularly assess their behavior and its impact on others, staying vigilant against the onset of harmful tendencies.

2. Understand Stressors and Triggers: Identifying personal stressors and triggers that can lead to toxic behaviors is

essential. Understanding these can help leaders develop coping strategies and maintain a healthy leadership style.

3. Build a Strong Support Network: Having a network of peers, mentors, and advisors is invaluable. This network provides perspective, feedback, and support, helping leaders navigate challenges and stay grounded.

4. Maintain Work-Life Balance: Preventing burnout through a healthy work-life balance is crucial. Engaging in activities outside of work, like hobbies and spending time with loved ones, contributes to a leader's overall well-being.

5. Continuous Learning and Development: Ongoing training in areas such as ethical leadership and emotional intelligence is vital. Such education helps leaders build the skills necessary to lead effectively and empathetically.

6. Encourage Open Communication: Creating an environment where feedback is encouraged and valued is key to early detection of toxic behaviors. This openness helps in addressing issues before they escalate.

7. Practice Empathy and Humility: Leaders should strive to understand and value their team's perspectives, fostering a culture of inclusivity and support.

8. Proactive Correction of Toxic Behaviors: If toxic traits begin to surface, leaders must take immediate action to rectify their course. This might involve seeking professional guidance or making substantial changes in their approach and behavior.

9. Professional Help May Be Necessary: Recognizing when to seek external help, such as coaching or counseling, is important. Professional guidance can provide leaders with the tools and strategies to overcome toxic tendencies.

These takeaways emphasize that preventing and mitigating toxic leadership is an ongoing process that requires commitment, self-reflection, and a willingness to change. By focusing on these key areas, leaders can ensure they maintain a positive influence on their teams and organizations, fostering a healthy and productive work environment.

As we conclude this chapter, the emphasis falls strongly on the importance of proactive measures in both leadership and organizational culture to prevent the descent into toxic behavior patterns. This critical theme underscores the reality that leadership is not just about achieving goals and driving success but equally about how these objectives are pursued and the impact on the people involved. Leadership transcends mere management of tasks and people; it's fundamentally about nurturing an environment of respect, integrity, and positive growth. Proactive measures, therefore, are not just reactive strategies to counteract negative tendencies but are integral to the very fabric of effective leadership. They involve constant vigilance, a commitment to personal and professional growth, and a deep sense of responsibility towards the health and well-being of the organizational culture.

It's crucial for leaders to recognize that their actions and decisions have a ripple effect, influencing the behavior of others and shaping the organizational ethos. Creating a culture where ethical practices, empathy, and open communication are not just encouraged but exemplified by leadership sets the tone for the entire organization. It fosters an environment where employees feel valued, respected, and motivated to contribute their best. Moreover, in an era where organizational success is increasingly measured not just in financial terms but also by the well-being of its workforce, the role of leadership becomes even more pivotal. Proactive measures in leadership are about anticipating challenges, understanding the human element in every decision, and ensuring that the pursuit of success does not compromise ethical standards or the quality of the work environment.

In essence, this chapter highlights that the path to effective leadership and a healthy organizational culture is paved with continuous self-awareness, empathy, ethical conduct, and a commitment to fostering a positive work environment. These are not just ideals but practical necessities for sustainable success in today's complex and dynamic business landscape. As leaders navigate their roles, keeping these principles at the forefront ensures that they not only achieve their goals but do so in a way that upholds the dignity and well-being of those they lead.

Chapter 3: "Tales from the Dark Side: Real-World Villains"

Chapter 3 takes us on a journey through the annals of business history, presenting real-life case studies of notorious leaders whose actions left indelible marks on their organizations and industries. This chapter sets the stage for a compelling exploration of leadership gone awry, delving into the stories of leaders who, for various reasons, deviated from the paths of ethical and effective management. As we introduce these real-world villains, the chapter aims not just to recount tales of leadership failures but to dissect the circumstances, decisions, and consequences that defined these notorious figures. Through these case studies, we gain insights into the complexities of leadership and the fine line that often exists between assertive decision-making and unethical behavior.

Each story serves as a cautionary tale, highlighting the potential risks and repercussions of toxic leadership. By examining these real-life examples, readers can glean valuable lessons about the importance of ethical decision-making, the impact of leadership on organizational culture, and the long-term consequences of ignoring the principles of responsible management. These tales also serve as powerful reminders of the responsibilities that come with leadership roles. They underscore the need for constant self-awareness, accountability, and a steadfast commitment to ethical practices. In a world where the pressures of performance, competition, and success can be overwhelming, these stories are a sobering reminder of what can happen when leaders lose sight of their moral compasses.

Case Study One: "The Autocratic Titan"

Is the story of a leader whose name became synonymous with authoritarian tactics in the corporate world: Robert Nardelli, former CEO of Home Depot. Nardelli's tenure at Home Depot, from December 2000 to January 2007, provides a striking example of how autocratic leadership can impact a major organization.

Nardelli came to Home Depot with a background from General Electric and brought with him a highly structured, centralized management style. He overhauled Home Depot's decentralized management, imposing a strict, top-down approach. Under his leadership, decision-making was consolidated, with senior managers having to adhere closely to directives from the top.

While this approach brought initial financial gains – under Nardelli, Home Depot saw significant growth in sales and operations – it also led to growing discontent within the company. Nardelli's autocratic style was marked by a focus on financial metrics and operational efficiency, often at the cost of employee morale and customer service, which had been the cornerstone of Home Depot's success.

One of the critical issues was Nardelli's handling of human resources. He replaced knowledgeable floor staff with less experienced and lower-paid workers, a move that saved costs but diminished the quality of customer service. This decision, among others, led to a significant decline in customer satisfaction and damaged the company's once-stellar reputation in this area.

Nardelli's leadership style was seen as imperious and dismissive of dissenting views. His approach stifled innovation and initiative among employees, leading to a culture of compliance rather than creativity. Internal communication suffered, and the company's once vibrant and participative corporate culture began to erode.

The culmination of these issues became evident when, despite the financial growth, Home Depot's stock price stagnated and then fell. This decline was a reflection of the market's lack of confidence in the long-term sustainability of Nardelli's leadership approach. His eventual departure from the company with a substantial severance package was met with widespread criticism and has since been used as an example of poor corporate governance.

Nardelli's tenure at Home Depot serves as a cautionary tale of the risks associated with autocratic leadership in an environment that traditionally thrived on employee empowerment and customer satisfaction. This case study underscores the importance of balancing operational efficiency with people management and the need for leaders to adapt their styles to the culture and values of their organizations.

The impact of Robert Nardelli's autocratic leadership style at Home Depot had significant and multifaceted implications, both for the organization and its employees. Nardelli's tenure, while initially bringing financial growth, eventually led to a series of negative outcomes that highlighted the risks associated with an authoritarian approach in an environment previously known for its employee empowerment and customer-centric culture. The impact on the organization was profound including:

- Financial Performance: Initially, Nardelli's focus on operational efficiency and expansion strategies led to increased sales and expansion of the business. However, this financial growth was overshadowed by the stagnation and subsequent decline of the company's stock price, reflecting market skepticism about the sustainability of his approach.

- Customer Satisfaction: One of the most significant impacts was the decline in customer satisfaction. Nardelli's decision to replace experienced floor staff with less knowledgeable employees, while cost-effective, severely affected the quality of customer service, which had been a key differentiator for Home Depot.

- Reputational Damage: The company, once renowned for its excellent customer service and knowledgeable staff, saw its reputation suffer. This decline in reputation had long-term implications for the brand and its competitive position in the market.

- Corporate Governance Concerns: Nardelli's hefty severance package upon his departure, despite the company's underperforming stock, raised questions about corporate governance and executive compensation practices, further tarnishing the company's image.

- Employee Morale: Nardelli's top-down management style and the undermining of the decentralized management model significantly impacted employee morale. The culture shifted from one of empowerment and engagement to one of compliance and disillusionment.

- Loss of Company Culture: The shift in corporate culture from an inclusive and employee-focused environment to a more authoritarian one led to a loss of the company's original spirit. This change was demotivating for many employees, especially those who had been with the company since its early days.

- Reduced Innovation and Creativity: The autocratic leadership style stifled innovation and creativity among employees. With a reduced emphasis on employee input and initiative, the company struggled to foster and maintain a culture of innovation.

- Increased Turnover: The combination of reduced employee morale, changes in compensation structures, and a shift in company culture likely contributed to increased turnover rates, as employees sought more fulfilling work environments elsewhere.

Nardelli's tenure at Home Depot demonstrates the profound impact that leadership style can have on both an organization's financial performance and its internal culture. While an authoritarian approach might bring short-term operational efficiencies, it can also lead to long-term damage in terms of employee engagement, customer satisfaction, and overall corporate reputation. This case underscores the importance of leadership that balances operational excellence with a deep understanding and appreciation of company culture and employee welfare.

Case Study Two: "The Manipulative Visionary"

The intriguing and cautionary tale of Elizabeth Holmes, the founder and CEO of Theranos. Holmes's story is a striking example of a leader using manipulation and deceit under the guise of visionary goals, highlighting the dangerous confluence of unchecked ambition, innovation, and unethical leadership.

Elizabeth Holmes emerged in the healthcare industry with a bold vision to revolutionize blood testing. She promised a groundbreaking technology that could conduct a wide array of tests with just a few drops of blood, a concept that quickly captured the imagination of investors, the media, and the public. Her compelling narrative, marked by charisma and persuasive eloquence, drew significant attention and investment to Theranos.

However, beneath this veneer of groundbreaking innovation lay a starkly different reality. The technology Holmes championed was fundamentally flawed and failed to deliver on its lofty promises. Despite this, Holmes continued to advocate for and raise substantial funds for her product, engaging in a pattern of manipulation and deceit.

The repercussions of Holmes's leadership at Theranos were extensive and severe. Investors and partners were misled by her fabrications, leading to financial losses and a significant erosion of trust. More alarmingly, the unreliability of Theranos's blood testing technology posed grave risks to patient health, with the potential for misdiagnoses and inappropriate medical treatments stemming from inaccurate test results.

The working environment at Theranos further mirrored the ethical compromises at its helm. Employees were frequently placed in positions where they were compelled to either partake in the deceit or leave the company. This created a workplace rife with moral dilemmas and plummeting morale.

Beyond its immediate sphere, the Theranos scandal profoundly impacted public trust, casting a shadow of skepticism over startups and innovation in the healthcare sector. It called into question the regulatory oversight of medical technologies, underscoring the need for more stringent checks and balances in the industry.

Holmes's journey from a visionary to a manipulative leader culminated in legal battles, facing charges of massive fraud. This legal reckoning brought to the fore the critical importance of ethical leadership and accountability.

The story of Elizabeth Holmes as a "Manipulative Visionary" serves as a stark reminder of the importance of ethical conduct in leadership. It exemplifies the catastrophic consequences of allowing ambition to overshadow integrity and emphasizes the necessity for leaders to uphold honesty and transparency, particularly in sectors where the stakes are life-altering. Her case reinforces the vital role of ethical decision-making in sustaining trust and credibility in the business world.

The consequences of Elizabeth Holmes's leadership at Theranos for team morale and organizational integrity were profound and multifaceted. Her approach, characterized by manipulation and deceit, created a ripple effect that severely impacted both the internal dynamics of the team and the broader ethical fabric of the organization.

In terms of team morale, the work environment at Theranos became increasingly strained and toxic. Employees, many of whom were initially drawn to the company by Holmes's vision and the promise of revolutionary healthcare technology, found themselves in a workplace steeped in secrecy and fear. As the truth about the technology's shortcomings began to emerge internally, employees faced moral dilemmas. Those who raised concerns or questioned the technology's efficacy were often marginalized or dismissed, leading to a culture where honest communication and feedback were stifled.

This atmosphere eroded trust among team members and towards leadership. The constant pressure to conform to the company's public narrative, despite its discrepancies with reality, created an environment of mutual suspicion and low morale. Talented employees who valued integrity and transparency found themselves in an untenable situation, leading to high turnover and a loss of valuable expertise.

The impact on organizational integrity was equally damaging. Theranos, under Holmes's leadership, had built its brand on the promise of innovation and integrity in healthcare. However, the unfolding of events revealed a stark contrast between the company's public image and its actual practices. This discrepancy damaged the company's reputation, leading to a loss of credibility in the eyes of customers, partners, and the broader public.

The fallout from Holmes's actions extended beyond internal operations to the wider stakeholder community. Investors, who had placed their trust and resources in Theranos, faced significant financial losses and reputational damage. Partners who had aligned themselves with the company's vision of revolutionizing healthcare found themselves embroiled in controversy. The implications for the healthcare industry were also significant, as Theranos's story became a cautionary tale about the importance of due diligence and ethical compliance in healthcare innovation.

The leadership saga at Theranos under Elizabeth Holmes illustrates how the actions of a single leader can profoundly impact both team morale and organizational integrity. It highlights the critical importance of ethical leadership and the need for a corporate culture that values transparency, honesty, and open communication. The Theranos case serves as a reminder that the long-term success and sustainability of an organization are intrinsically tied to its commitment to ethical practices and its ability to foster a supportive and honest work environment.

Case Study Three: "The Charismatic Destroyer"

Examines the tumultuous tenure of Kenneth Lay, former CEO of Enron. Lay's leadership at Enron is a classic example of how a charismatic leader can leave a trail of destruction in their wake, leading one of the most infamous corporate collapses in history.

Kenneth Lay founded Enron in 1985 and quickly transformed it into an energy behemoth, known for its innovation in energy trading. Lay was charismatic and well-respected, known for his ability to charm investors, employees, and the public. Under his leadership, Enron was hailed as a model of corporate success and innovation. However, beneath the surface of this success lay a fundamentally flawed and unethical corporate strategy. Lay and his executives engaged in complex accounting fraud to hide the company's mounting debts and inflate its profits. This manipulation created an illusion of a highly profitable company, driving up the stock price and enriching Lay and other executives through stock options. The impact of Lay's leadership on Enron was catastrophic:

- Financial Collapse: The accounting fraud eventually unraveled, leading to Enron's bankruptcy in 2001. This collapse wiped out thousands of jobs, decimated employee retirement plans, and led to significant financial losses for investors.

- Cultural Decay: Lay's leadership fostered a culture of greed and ethical compromise. The relentless pursuit of profit and stock price performance above all else led employees to engage in risky and unethical practices.

- Legal and Regulatory Fallout: The Enron scandal led to numerous legal battles. Lay himself faced charges of fraud and conspiracy, though he passed away before sentencing. The scandal also prompted significant changes in corporate governance and accounting standards, including the Sarbanes-Oxley Act.

- Loss of Trust: Enron's collapse had a profound impact on public trust in corporate America. It raised questions about the integrity of corporate leadership and the efficacy of regulatory oversight.

Kenneth Lay's story as "The Charismatic Destroyer" at Enron serves as a powerful lesson in the dangers of charismatic leadership when it is not grounded in ethical and transparent practices. It underscores the importance of integrity in leadership and the devastating consequences when it is absent. Lay's legacy at Enron reminds us that effective leadership is not just about vision and charisma; it's equally about ethical stewardship and accountability.

The paradox of charm and damage in leadership, as vividly illustrated by Kenneth Lay's tenure at Enron, encapsulates a complex and often misleading facet of leadership dynamics. This paradox emerges when a leader's charisma, which can be a powerful tool for motivation and inspiration, intertwines with unethical decision-making, ultimately leading to detrimental consequences.

Charm in leadership is often characterized by a compelling charisma, persuasive communication skills, and an ability to emotionally connect with people. These traits are highly beneficial in rallying teams, attracting investors, and crafting a compelling vision for the future. Leaders like Kenneth Lay are typically admired for their confidence and clarity of direction, making them exceptionally effective in gaining support and commitment. However, this charm becomes paradoxical and potentially dangerous when it serves as a facade for unethical practices. In the case of Enron, Lay's charismatic leadership was pivotal in establishing the company's public image and convincing stakeholders of its robust financial health and innovative business strategies. Beneath this surface, however, lay a reality of widespread accounting fraud and risky business behaviors.

The damage caused by such paradoxical leadership extends across multiple dimensions. Organizational collapse is often a significant consequence, as was the case with Enron, leading to substantial financial and reputational damage. The impact of such leadership on organizational culture is profound, creating an environment where unethical behavior is normalized and even encouraged. Employees, under the influence of a charismatic leader, might mirror these harmful behaviors, leading to a widespread decline in ethical standards within the organization.

The repercussions of a leader's unethical actions are far-reaching, impacting not just the organization but also its employees, investors, customers, and the broader industry. The aftermath includes job losses, eroded life savings, and a deep-seated mistrust in corporate governance. Legal battles and regulatory changes often follow, as seen in the regulatory aftermath of the Enron scandal.

The story of Kenneth Lay at Enron serves as a critical lesson on the importance of ethical integrity in leadership. It underscores the need for mechanisms that keep charismatic leadership in check, ensuring that the persuasive abilities of leaders are coupled with ethical and transparent practices. This paradox highlights the essential role of accountability and ethical stewardship in leadership, emphasizing that the charisma which builds companies should not be allowed to become the catalyst for their downfall.

Diversity in destructive leadership sheds light on the varied faces of dark leadership across different industries and cultures. This diversity demonstrates that toxic leadership behaviors are not confined to any specific sector or cultural context; they can emerge anywhere, influenced by a range of factors including industry norms, cultural expectations, organizational structures, and personal attributes of the leaders themselves.

In various industries, the manifestation of dark leadership can differ significantly.

The Financial Sector

Destructive leadership often revolves around excessive risk-taking, financial manipulation, and a ruthless focus on short-term profits. Driven by the high-stakes nature of the industry, leaders may engage in unethical practices like fraud or insider trading, driven by the pressure to deliver extraordinary financial returns.

The Technology Industry

Destructive leadership might take the form of relentless drive for innovation at the expense of ethical considerations. This can include overworking employees, ignoring safety standards in product development, or using customer data unethically. The fast-paced, high-pressure environment of tech startups often exacerbates these tendencies.

Manufacturing and Retail

In these sectors, destructive leadership might manifest in the exploitation of labor, disregard for environmental standards, or cutting corners in product quality and safety. The pressure to reduce costs and increase efficiency can drive leaders to make decisions that adversely affect workers and consumers.

Healthcare and Pharmaceuticals

Destructive leadership can have dire consequences, including compromising patient care for profits, pushing drugs to market without adequate testing, or engaging in unethical marketing practices. The balance between profitability and patient welfare is a key ethical challenge in these industries.

Culturally, the expression of destructive leadership can also vary. In cultures that highly value hierarchy and respect for authority, destructive leadership might manifest as authoritarianism, where leaders expect absolute obedience and dissent is not tolerated. In cultures with a high emphasis on collective success and harmony, destructive leadership might be subtler, involving manipulation or passive-aggressive tactics to maintain control and appearances. In individualistic cultures, destructive leadership might lean towards narcissism, where leaders prioritize their own success and image over the well-being of the organization and its people.

Despite these variations, common threads in destructive leadership include a lack of empathy, ethical flexibility, and a focus on personal or immediate gains over long-term welfare and sustainability. Understanding the diversity in destructive leadership is crucial for organizations as it helps in developing targeted strategies to prevent and address these behaviors. This includes cultural awareness, industry-specific ethical training, and policies and practices that discourage toxic leadership behaviors and encourage a healthy, inclusive, and ethical work environment.

Diversity in destructive leadership across various industries and cultures offers a range of lessons that are invaluable for organizations aiming to foster healthy leadership and prevent toxic behaviors. From each unique scenario, we can extract key insights:

- In the financial sector, where destructive leadership often manifests as unethical risk-taking and financial manipulation, the lesson is the importance of robust regulatory compliance and ethical financial practices. Organizations need to emphasize transparency and accountability, ensuring that the pursuit of profit does not override ethical considerations.

- In the technology industry, where relentless innovation can sometimes lead to ethical lapses, the key lesson is balancing the drive for technological advancement with social responsibility. This includes prioritizing employee well-being, ethical use of data, and considering the broader impact of technological innovations on society.

- Manufacturing and retail sectors, often grappling with issues around labor exploitation and environmental disregard, teach us the value of sustainable and ethical operational practices. These industries highlight the necessity of maintaining ethical supply chains, fair labor practices, and environmental stewardship.

- The healthcare and pharmaceutical industries, where the consequences of toxic leadership can directly impact patient welfare, underscore the need for a patient-centered approach in leadership. This includes prioritizing patient safety over profits, ensuring rigorous testing of products, and ethical marketing practices.

Culturally, scenarios vary widely. In cultures with hierarchical values, the lesson is about the importance of fostering open communication and encouraging diverse perspectives, mitigating the risks associated with authoritarian leadership. In cultures that emphasize collective success, it's crucial to cultivate an environment where individual voices are heard, and constructive dissent is valued, preventing manipulative or passive-aggressive leadership styles. In individualistic cultures, where narcissistic leadership traits might prevail, the focus should be on team success and collaborative achievements. This involves promoting a culture where individual accomplishments contribute to and are aligned with the organization's goals and values.

These lessons, drawn from a diverse range of scenarios, highlight a common theme: the importance of ethical, empathetic, and inclusive leadership. They emphasize the need for organizations to be vigilant in recognizing and addressing toxic leadership traits, irrespective of industry or cultural context. By learning from these scenarios, organizations can develop strategies to promote a leadership culture that is not only effective but also responsible and attuned to the welfare of all stakeholders.

The impact of toxic leadership extends far beyond the individual leader, permeating various facets of their organizations and even influencing entire industries. Let's look into the broader effects of destructive leaders, highlighting how toxic actions and behavior can have far-reaching consequences.

Toxic leaders profoundly affect the culture of their organizations. Their leadership style can instill a culture of fear, reduce morale, and stifle innovation and creativity. Employees under toxic leadership often experience increased stress, job dissatisfaction, and a decline in mental and physical health. High turnover rates are common as employees leave in search of healthier work environments. Beyond impacting employee morale, toxic leadership can also affect the financial and operational aspects of a business. Decisions made without regard for ethical considerations or sustainability can lead to short-term gains but often result in long-term harm, including financial losses, diminished shareholder value, and a tarnished brand reputation.

The impact of toxic leadership extends to customer and client relationships. Unethical practices or a decline in product or service quality can erode customer trust and loyalty, leading to a loss of business and damaging the organization's public image and reputation. Destructive leaders often engage in practices that skirt or violate regulations, leading to legal challenges and regulatory scrutiny. This can have significant financial implications, including fines and penalties, and can consume considerable management attention and resources.

The actions of toxic leaders can extend beyond their organizations, affecting entire industries. They can contribute to a lack of trust in the industry, influence regulatory changes, and set negative examples that might inadvertently be followed by others in the industry. In the long term, toxic leadership can stifle innovation within the organization. A culture that does not encourage risk-taking or values only short-term results can lag in innovation, affecting the organization's competitive position in the market.

Toxic leadership can hinder the development of future leaders within the organization. Moreover, it can make it challenging to attract top talent, as prospective employees are more cautious about joining organizations with a reputation for poor leadership. The impact of toxic leadership is far-reaching, affecting not just the immediate team but the entire organization and even the broader industry. Understanding these broader effects is crucial for organizations, emphasizing the need for vigilant leadership selection, continuous monitoring, and the cultivation of a positive, ethical organizational culture. Addressing toxic leadership is not just about rectifying individual behavior but about fostering an environment where such behavior is recognized, challenged, and not allowed to take root.

The ripple effect of toxic leadership on stakeholders, employees, and markets is significant and multifaceted, illustrating how the influence of a leader extends well beyond their immediate decisions and actions. When it comes to stakeholders, including investors, partners, and shareholders, toxic leadership can severely damage trust and confidence. Investors and shareholders may see their values and expectations misaligned with the organization's actions, leading to a loss of financial investment and support. Partners may find their reputations at risk due to association, causing them to reconsider or sever their ties.

Employees bear a considerable brunt of the impact of toxic leadership. Beyond the immediate stress and unhappiness, such leadership can lead to a demoralized workforce, high turnover rates, and a tarnished employer brand, making it difficult to attract and retain talent. The long-term implications include a loss of institutional knowledge, reduced productivity, and a decline in innovation, as employees become disengaged and less inclined to contribute their best ideas.

For markets and consumers, the effects of toxic leadership can manifest in diminished trust in the brand. Customers and clients might start associating the organization with unethical practices or poor quality products and services, leading to a loss of market share. In some cases, the entire industry can be affected, especially if the toxic leadership prompts increased regulatory scrutiny and changes in industry standards or practices. Furthermore, toxic leadership can impact the broader community and society. Unethical business practices can have social, environmental, and economic repercussions, contributing to larger issues like economic inequality, environmental degradation, or societal mistrust in business institutions.

The ripple effect of toxic leadership underscores the interconnectedness of business leadership with multiple facets of society and the economy. It highlights the crucial responsibility leaders hold, not just to their organizations but to a wider network of stakeholders, and underscores the need for ethical, empathetic, and responsible leadership.

Learning from the Dark Side of leadership involves extracting key lessons and warnings from various case studies of toxic leadership. These lessons are vital for organizations and leaders committed to fostering ethical, sustainable, and positive work environments.

One of the primary lessons is the critical importance of ethical leadership. The case studies demonstrate how a lack of ethics and disregard for moral standards can lead to disastrous outcomes, not just for the leaders themselves but for entire organizations. Ethical leadership should be a fundamental pillar in any organization's culture, and leaders must be held accountable to these standards. Another key takeaway is the significance of transparent and honest communication within organizations. Many of the issues arising from toxic leadership could have been mitigated or even avoided if there had been open channels for honest dialogue and feedback. Creating a culture where employees feel safe to voice concerns and where transparency is valued is essential.

The impact of leadership on organizational culture is also a crucial lesson. Leaders set the tone for the workplace environment, and their behavior, values, and attitudes are often mirrored by employees. A toxic leader can corrupt the entire culture, emphasizing the need for leaders who are not only skilled and competent but also empathetic, supportive, and inclusive. These case studies highlight the necessity of robust checks and balances within organizations. Effective governance structures, including clear policies, regular audits, and accountability mechanisms, are essential in preventing and addressing toxic leadership.

The importance of stakeholder consideration is another lesson. Leaders must recognize their responsibility not just to shareholders but to a broader range of stakeholders, including employees, customers, and the community. Decisions should be made with a holistic view of their impact. Lastly, learning from the dark side underscores the need for ongoing vigilance and self-reflection in leadership. Leaders should continuously assess their actions and their impact, seeking feedback and engaging in self-improvement. This vigilance is key to ensuring that they do not inadvertently slip into destructive patterns of behavior.

The lessons from these case studies of toxic leadership are clear: ethical leadership, transparent communication, positive organizational culture, effective governance, stakeholder consideration, and ongoing self-assessment are all critical in preventing and addressing the dark side of leadership. These lessons serve as warnings and guides for current and future leaders, reminding them of the profound impact their leadership can have.

Preventing similar scenarios in one's leadership journey involves adopting strategies that emphasize ethical behavior, self-awareness, and proactive organizational practices. These strategies are designed to help leaders navigate their roles responsibly and effectively, avoiding the pitfalls of toxic leadership. As we have mentioned several times, prioritizing ethical leadership is foundational and crucial. This involves not only adhering to ethical norms and standards but also embedding these values into the organizational culture. Leaders should lead by example, demonstrating integrity and fairness in all decisions and actions.

Fostering an environment of open and honest communication is essential. Leaders should encourage feedback from all levels of the organization and create safe spaces where employees feel comfortable voicing concerns or challenges. This open dialogue can help identify potential issues early and foster a culture of trust. Self-awareness is a key aspect of effective leadership. Regular self-reflection, perhaps through feedback mechanisms like 360-degree reviews or self-assessment tools, helps leaders understand their impact on others and identify any areas for improvement.

Implementing robust governance structures is also vital. This includes clear policies and procedures that outline acceptable behaviors and practices, along with mechanisms for accountability. Regular training and development opportunities can also reinforce ethical practices and leadership skills. Maintaining a focus on the well-being of employees is important. Leaders should strive to create a balanced work environment where employees feel valued and supported. This includes recognizing the signs of stress or burnout and addressing them proactively.

Developing a strong support network can provide leaders with guidance and perspective. This network might include mentors, peers, or professional coaches who can offer advice, share experiences, and provide an outside perspective on challenges and decisions. Leaders should be prepared to take decisive action if toxic behaviors or situations arise. This might involve difficult decisions, such as restructuring teams, changing leadership styles, or even parting ways with individuals who consistently exhibit harmful behaviors.

By adopting these strategies, leaders can navigate their journey more effectively, steering clear of the behaviors and practices that lead to toxic leadership. The focus should always be on leading with integrity, empathy, and a commitment to the betterment of the team and organization. It's essential to reflect on the critical importance of recognizing and countering destructive leadership. The case studies and discussions presented highlight how toxic leadership can insidiously erode the foundations of an organization, affecting not just its immediate success but also its long-term viability and the well-being of its employees.

The importance of recognizing destructive leadership lies in its subtlety and the often gradual manner in which it manifests. It requires vigilance, awareness, and a willingness to acknowledge that even well-intentioned leadership can deviate towards harmful practices. Early recognition of these tendencies is key to preventing the wide-ranging negative impacts that can ensue.

Countering destructive leadership is equally crucial and demands a proactive approach. It involves cultivating a culture of ethical practices, transparency, and open communication. Leaders play a pivotal role in this process, as they set the tone and standards for behavior within their organizations. By embodying ethical principles and fostering an environment of mutual respect and accountability, leaders can mitigate the risks associated with toxic leadership. Organizations must have robust mechanisms in place to address toxic behaviors. This includes clear policies, regular training, and effective channels for feedback and reporting. Creating an environment where ethical concerns can be raised without fear of retribution is essential for maintaining a healthy organizational culture.

The journey through the darker aspects of leadership serves as a vital reminder of the responsibilities that come with a leadership role. It underscores the need for continuous self-assessment, commitment to ethical practices, and the creation of supportive and inclusive work environments. Recognizing and countering destructive leadership is not just a task for individual leaders but a collective responsibility that involves everyone within an organization. By staying vigilant and committed to positive leadership practices, organizations can thrive and foster environments where employees feel valued, respected, and motivated to contribute their best.

As we conclude this chapter, the focus shifts to the importance of proactive leadership development as a means to avoid the pitfalls of destructive leadership. The journey through various examples of toxic leadership underscores that preventing such scenarios isn't merely about averting negative behaviors, but more importantly, about cultivating positive, ethical, and effective leadership practices.

Proactive leadership development involves a commitment to continuous learning and improvement. Leaders should be encouraged to engage in ongoing training and education, focusing not just on technical skills but also on areas like emotional intelligence, ethical decision-making, and effective communication. This holistic approach to development ensures that leaders are well-equipped to handle the complexities of their roles in a balanced and ethically sound manner.

Creating opportunities for mentorship and coaching is another crucial aspect. Experienced mentors can provide guidance, share insights, and help emerging leaders navigate challenges while maintaining ethical standards. Coaching, whether it's peer-based or professional, offers a platform for leaders to explore their leadership style, understand their impact on others, and develop strategies to enhance their effectiveness.

Organizations should also foster a culture of open feedback and self-reflection. Encouraging leaders to seek and thoughtfully consider feedback from their teams can provide valuable insights into their leadership style and its effects on others. Self-reflection is a powerful tool for personal growth, helping leaders to recognize their strengths and areas for improvement. It's important for organizations to establish and reinforce ethical norms and values. These should be clearly communicated and embedded in all aspects of the organization, from decision-making processes to day-to-day operations. Leaders play a key role in embodying and upholding these values, setting an example for their teams. Proactive leadership development means preparing leaders to recognize and address the early signs of toxic behavior, both in themselves and in others. This involves creating an environment where such issues can be discussed openly and addressed constructively.

The key to avoiding the pitfalls of destructive leadership lies in proactive leadership development. By investing in the growth and ethical grounding of leaders, organizations can cultivate a leadership culture that not only drives success but does so with integrity and respect for the well-being of all stakeholders. This approach ensures that the organization not only thrives in the present but is also sustainable and respected in the long term.

Chapter 4: "Escape from the Underworld: Overthrowing Darth Vader"

This chapter is dedicated to identifying the signs and patterns of destructive leadership and understanding its profound impact on individuals and organizations. We shift our focus to the early detection of destructive leadership behaviors. Recognizing these signs is not always straightforward, as they can be subtle and insidious, often masquerading as strong or decisive leadership. The chapter discusses various indicators of destructive leadership, which may include consistent patterns of unethical decisions, a disregard for the well-being of employees, manipulation, and a tendency to foster a culture of fear and intimidation.

We also examine the varied manifestations of destructive leadership. This might range from overt aggression and hostility to more covert tactics like manipulation and passive-aggressive behaviors. Understanding these patterns is crucial for early intervention and prevention. The chapter further explores the impact of such leadership on individuals within the organization. Destructive leadership can lead to a toxic work environment, characterized by high stress, low morale, and a general sense of insecurity among employees. This environment not only hampers individual well-being and productivity but can also lead to broader organizational issues such as high turnover rates, a decline in employee engagement, and damage to the organization's reputation.

We also explore the wider implications of destructive leadership on the organization as a whole. This includes a discussion on how such leadership can stifle innovation, erode trust, and create a dysfunctional organizational culture. The long-term sustainability of the organization can be severely compromised under the shadow of destructive leadership.

Chapter 4 is an essential guide for recognizing the often-subtle signs of destructive leadership and understanding its far-reaching implications. This chapter serves as a foundational piece for the following sections, which will explore strategies for addressing and transforming destructive leadership into positive and effective leadership practices.

Strategies for individuals to build resilience against negative leadership influences are essential for maintaining personal well-being and professional efficacy in challenging work environments. To safeguard against the impacts of destructive leadership, individuals can adopt several key strategies. Developing a strong personal support network is crucial. This network can include colleagues, mentors, friends, and family who provide emotional support, advice, and a sounding board for experiences at work. Having people to discuss challenges with can help individuals maintain perspective and reduce feelings of isolation.

Cultivating personal resilience is another vital strategy. This involves developing coping mechanisms to manage stress and adversity, such as engaging in regular physical activity, practicing mindfulness or meditation, and pursuing hobbies and interests outside of work. These activities can provide a much-needed respite from workplace stress. Setting clear professional and personal boundaries is also important. Understanding and articulating one's limits in terms of workload, working hours, and emotional labor can help prevent burnout and maintain a healthy work-life balance.

Seeking professional development opportunities can empower individuals to feel more in control of their careers. This could involve pursuing additional training, attending workshops, or simply staying informed about industry trends and best practices. Gaining new skills and knowledge can boost confidence and open up alternative career paths. Staying ethically grounded is essential.

This means being clear about one's own values and principles and standing by them, even in the face of negative leadership. This commitment to personal ethics can serve as a guiding light in difficult situations.

Practicing assertive communication is also beneficial. Being able to communicate one's thoughts, feelings, and needs effectively and respectfully can help in navigating challenging interactions with leaders and colleagues. Being aware of organizational policies and resources is important. Knowing the available channels for reporting unethical behavior or seeking support, such as human resources or employee assistance programs, can provide a recourse in difficult situations. By implementing these strategies, individuals can build resilience against the negative influences of destructive leadership. This resilience is key not just for surviving challenging work environments but also for thriving professionally and personally, regardless of the external circumstances.

Organizational policies and practices play a crucial role in fostering resilience among employees, especially in environments where they may be exposed to negative leadership influences. By implementing thoughtful and supportive policies, organizations can create a work environment that not only mitigates the effects of destructive leadership but also promotes the well-being and growth of its workforce.

One key policy is the establishment of clear channels for feedback and reporting. This includes creating mechanisms for employees to safely report unethical behavior or leadership concerns without fear of retribution. Such channels should be well-publicized and easily accessible to all employees. Implementing comprehensive training programs that focus on ethical leadership, emotional intelligence, and conflict resolution is another essential practice. These programs should be designed to equip leaders and employees with the skills needed to navigate and address challenging workplace dynamics constructively.

Organizational policies should also emphasize the importance of work-life balance. This can be achieved through flexible work arrangements, reasonable workload expectations, and policies that encourage employees to take necessary breaks and vacation time. Creating a culture of open communication is vital. Organizations should encourage regular check-ins and open dialogues between managers and their teams. This practice helps in building trust, understanding individual challenges, and providing support where needed.

Organizational resilience can be further bolstered by providing access to mental health resources. This could include employee assistance programs, counseling services, and initiatives that focus on mental health awareness and support. Promoting diversity and inclusivity within the workplace is also key. A diverse and inclusive environment helps in creating a more empathetic and supportive workplace where different perspectives are valued and respected. Recognition and reward systems that acknowledge not just business achievements, but also ethical behavior and positive team contributions can reinforce a culture of resilience. Such systems encourage employees to uphold organizational values and contribute to a positive work environment.

Organizations should regularly review and update their policies to ensure they remain relevant and effective in addressing current workplace challenges. This proactive approach demonstrates a commitment to the continuous improvement of the work environment and the well-being of its employees. By adopting these policies and practices, organizations can create a supportive framework that fosters resilience among employees, helping them to thrive even in the face of challenging leadership scenarios.

Encouraging transparent and honest communication in the workplace is fundamental for creating a trusting and open organizational culture. Here are some techniques that can help achieve this:

1. Leadership Example: Leaders should model transparency and honesty in their communication. By openly sharing

information, acknowledging mistakes, and communicating openly about company challenges and successes, leaders set a tone that encourages similar behavior throughout the organization.

2. Regular Open Forums and Meetings: Hosting regular meetings where employees at all levels are encouraged to speak openly and share their thoughts can foster a culture of open communication. These forums should be safe spaces where employees feel comfortable voicing their opinions without fear of negative consequences.

3. Feedback Mechanisms: Implementing formal and informal feedback mechanisms can encourage honest communication. This could include regular performance reviews, suggestion boxes, and employee surveys. Ensuring anonymity in these mechanisms can help in garnering more candid responses.

4. Training Programs: Offering training in effective communication, active listening, and conflict resolution can equip employees with the skills necessary for transparent and honest dialogue. Such training can help in breaking down barriers to open communication.

5. Encourage Questioning and Curiosity: Creating an environment where questioning and curiosity are valued can lead to more transparent communication. Encourage employees to ask questions and seek clarification when needed.

6. Clear Communication Policies: Having clear policies around communication that emphasize the importance of honesty and transparency is crucial. These policies should outline the expectations and the importance of ethical communication practices.

7. Two-Way Communication Channels: Establishing two-way communication channels where information flows both from the top down and the bottom up can encourage a more open

dialogue. Employees should feel that their voices are heard and valued at all levels of the organization.

8. Conflict Resolution Protocols: Transparent communication often brings disagreements and conflicts to the surface. Having clear conflict resolution protocols can help in addressing these disagreements constructively and openly.

9. Celebrating Transparency: Recognize and celebrate instances where honest and transparent communication has led to positive outcomes. This recognition can reinforce the value placed on open dialogue in the organization.

10. Building Relationships: Encouraging team-building activities and informal interactions among employees can strengthen relationships and trust, which are foundational for honest communication.

By incorporating these techniques, organizations can cultivate a culture where transparent and honest communication is the norm, leading to increased trust, better problem-solving, and a more cohesive work environment.

Addressing the fear and silence often associated with toxic leadership is a crucial step in transforming an unhealthy workplace culture into a positive and supportive environment. It begins with acknowledging and understanding the root causes of this fear and silence. Employees often fear retribution, job loss, or being marginalized for speaking up against negative behaviors or decisions of leaders.

Creating a safe and supportive environment where employees feel confident to voice their concerns without fear of negative consequences is essential. This involves establishing clear anti-retaliation policies and ensuring these policies are communicated effectively to all employees. It's important that staff understand their rights and the protections in place to support them. Leadership plays a key role in changing this culture of fear and silence. Leaders must lead by example, demonstrating openness to feedback and showing that they value honest communication. When leaders respond to feedback constructively and take visible actions based on it, it encourages a more open dialogue within the team. Training managers and supervisors in emotional intelligence, effective communication, and conflict resolution can also help. They often serve as the first point of contact for employees facing challenges and should be equipped to handle such situations sensitively and effectively.

Providing multiple channels for feedback and reporting concerns is another effective strategy. Apart from direct communication, anonymous feedback tools, suggestion boxes, or third-party reporting services can offer alternative avenues for employees to express their concerns. Regular check-ins and open forums can foster a culture of open dialogue. These meetings can provide opportunities for employees to discuss their challenges and concerns in a safe environment.

Encouraging collaboration and teamwork can also help break down the isolation often felt in toxic environments. Team-building activities and collaborative projects can foster a sense of community and mutual support among employees. It's important to recognize and address the symptoms of a toxic environment proactively. Regular surveys and assessments of employee satisfaction and workplace culture can help identify issues early and guide the development of targeted strategies to address them.

Organizations can move towards a culture where fear and silence are replaced with trust, openness, and mutual respect. This transformation is key not just for the well-being of employees but also for the overall health and success of the organization. Empowering employees to voice their concerns and contribute to solutions is essential for a healthy workplace culture. Various strategies can be employed to encourage open communication and ensure employees feel their voices are heard and valued.

Establishing regular and structured feedback channels, such as surveys or suggestion boxes, allows employees to share their thoughts and concerns. Ensuring anonymity can encourage more honest and open feedback. Additionally, hosting town hall meetings or open forums where employees can discuss issues and ideas with management fosters a sense of transparency and collaboration. These sessions should allow everyone an opportunity to speak and be heard.

Providing training in effective communication, assertiveness, and conflict resolution equips employees with the skills necessary to express their thoughts constructively. Leaders and managers play a crucial role in this process and should actively encourage employees to share their ideas and concerns. This can be achieved through regular one-on-one check-ins and team meetings, as well as public acknowledgment of the value of employee input.

Establishing employee advocacy or advisory groups can offer a formal avenue for employees to discuss workplace issues and propose solutions, acting as a liaison between the workforce and management. Implementing platforms or software for submitting ideas and suggestions for improvements can also stimulate innovation and provide employees with a direct avenue to contribute to organizational changes. Creating an environment of psychological safety, where employees feel safe to express themselves without fear of punishment or humiliation, is vital. This involves training, workshops, and consistent messaging from leadership about the importance of psychological safety.

Developing recognition programs that reward employees for speaking up and contributing ideas can reinforce a culture where employee input is valued. Pairing employees with mentors provides them with guidance and support in navigating workplace challenges and communicating effectively within the organization. Recognizing that different employees may prefer different modes of communication is important. Offering various options, such as in-person meetings, digital communication tools, or written feedback, accommodates diverse preferences and encourages wider participation.

By integrating these strategies, organizations can create a more open, inclusive, and dynamic workplace where every employee feels empowered to voice their concerns and contribute to the organization's success.

Case studies of organizations that have successfully reversed the effects of toxic leadership provide valuable insights into how deep-seated issues can be addressed and transformed into positive outcomes.

One notable example is Uber, which faced a major crisis in 2017 due to allegations of a toxic work culture under the leadership of its former CEO, Travis Kalanick. The company undertook significant changes after these issues came to light. This included the appointment of a new CEO, Dara Khosrowshahi, who implemented comprehensive cultural reforms. The changes focused on improving transparency, redefining company values, and establishing clearer guidelines for behavior. This cultural transformation effort also involved overhauling the leadership team and investing in diversity and inclusion initiatives. As a result, Uber started to rebuild its reputation and regain the trust of both its employees and customers.

Another example is General Motors (GM), which underwent a cultural shift under the leadership of CEO Mary Barra. When Barra took over, GM was plagued by a series of safety issues and a bureaucratic culture. Barra prioritized transparency and accountability, setting new standards for communication and decision-making within the organization. She led a cultural overhaul that emphasized customer safety and innovation, moving away from the traditional hierarchical and siloed approach. These efforts helped GM to improve its reputation, enhance employee engagement, and drive innovation.

Microsoft's transformation under CEO Satya Nadella also highlights how shifts in leadership and culture can reverse the effects of previous toxic leadership. When Nadella became CEO in 2014, he shifted the company's focus from rigid performance metrics to a growth mindset culture. This involved encouraging experimentation, learning from failures, and fostering a more collaborative and inclusive work environment. Under his leadership, Microsoft saw a revival in innovation, employee morale, and market performance, demonstrating how changing leadership style and organizational culture can lead to substantial business success.

These case studies illustrate that reversing the effects of toxic leadership is possible but requires committed and empathetic leadership, a willingness to confront and change entrenched cultural norms, and a sustained effort to rebuild trust and engagement among employees. Each of these companies shows that with the right approach, organizations can emerge stronger and more resilient from the challenges of toxic leadership.

Transforming a toxic work environment into a positive and supportive one is a challenging but crucial endeavor. This transformation requires a comprehensive approach that addresses the root causes of toxicity and fosters a culture of respect, collaboration, and well-being. The first step in this transformation is acknowledging the problem. Leadership must recognize and accept that there are issues within the organization that need to be addressed. This acknowledgment is crucial for setting the tone for change and demonstrating a commitment to improvement.

Conducting a thorough assessment of the current culture is essential. This can involve gathering feedback from employees through surveys, interviews, or focus groups to understand the specific issues and dynamics at play. This assessment should aim to identify patterns of negative behavior, sources of employee dissatisfaction, and areas where the organization falls short in terms of culture and values.

Developing a clear vision for the desired culture is the next step. This vision should outline the kind of work environment the organization aspires to create, focusing on values such as respect, integrity, transparency, and collaboration. Leadership should communicate this vision clearly and consistently to all employees. Implementing a plan of action based on the assessment and vision is critical. This plan should include specific, measurable steps to address identified issues. It might involve revising policies and procedures, implementing new training programs, restructuring teams, or making changes in leadership. Creating open channels for communication and feedback is vital. Employees should feel safe and encouraged to voice their concerns and contribute their ideas for improving the workplace. Regular check-ins, open forums, and anonymous feedback mechanisms can facilitate this communication.

Fostering a culture of accountability is essential. This means holding everyone, regardless of their position, accountable for their behavior. Toxic behavior should be addressed promptly and appropriately, demonstrating that negative actions have consequences. Investing in leadership development is also important. Leaders set the tone for the organization, so ensuring they have the skills and awareness to foster a positive culture is crucial. This might involve training in emotional intelligence, ethical leadership, and effective communication.

Monitoring progress and staying committed to continuous improvement is key. Cultural transformation is an ongoing process, and regular assessment of progress against the set vision and goals is necessary. Celebrating successes along the way can also help to maintain momentum and reinforce the commitment to a positive and supportive work environment.

Organizations can then leave a culture of toxicity and move towards a culture that promotes the well-being, engagement, and productivity of all employees.

The role of leadership in nurturing a healthy organizational culture is pivotal. Leaders are the primary drivers of culture within an organization, setting the tone for behavior, communication, and overall work environment. Their actions, decisions, and the values they embody and promote play a crucial role in shaping the organizational culture. Leaders are responsible for establishing and reinforcing the organization's core values and principles. They need to clearly articulate these values and ensure they are integrated into every aspect of the organization's operations, from decision-making processes to day-to-day interactions. By consistently demonstrating these values in their actions, leaders can embed them deeply within the organizational culture.

Communication is another critical aspect of a leader's role in shaping culture. Effective leaders communicate openly and transparently, fostering an environment of trust and openness. They encourage feedback and dialogue, making it safe for employees to express ideas and concerns. This open communication helps to create a culture of collaboration and continuous improvement.

Leaders also play a key role in modeling the behavior they expect from others. By embodying the behaviors that align with the organization's values, leaders set an example for all employees to follow. This includes showing respect, practicing empathy, and being accountable for their actions. They are instrumental in creating a positive and inclusive work environment. They should actively promote diversity and inclusion, ensuring that all employees feel valued and have equal opportunities. This involves not only policies and practices that support diversity but also fostering an environment where diverse perspectives are welcomed and respected.

Leadership needs to be proactive in identifying and addressing issues that can negatively impact the organizational culture. This includes dealing with toxic behavior, managing conflict effectively, and ensuring that the workplace is free from harassment and discrimination. Investing in the development and well-being of employees is a crucial aspect of nurturing a healthy culture. Leaders should provide opportunities for professional growth, support work-life balance, and create a supportive environment where employees can thrive. The role of leadership in nurturing a healthy organizational culture is multifaceted and vital. Leaders who effectively communicate, embody the organization's values, foster inclusivity, and invest in their employees' development can create a positive and productive work environment that benefits everyone in the organization.

Dealing with destructive leaders directly is a sensitive and challenging task, but it's crucial for preserving the health and integrity of an organization. There are a wide variety of tactics that can be employed starting with keeping a record of instances where the leader's behavior was destructive. This documentation should be factual, specific, and devoid of emotional language. It can be used to provide concrete examples during discussions or if formal action is required.

Before addressing the issue directly with the leader, seek advice and support from trusted colleagues, mentors, or HR professionals. They can provide perspective, suggest strategies, and help you prepare for the conversation. Arrange a private meeting to discuss your concerns. It's important to choose a time and place where the conversation can be conducted without interruptions and in a neutral environment.

When discussing specific behaviors, use "I" statements to describe how the leader's actions impact you and the team. This approach is less accusatory and more likely to lead to a productive conversation. It is important to be clear and specific about which behaviors are problematic and how they are impacting team morale, productivity, and the overall work environment. Avoid generalizations or personal attacks. Give the leader an opportunity to respond. Listen actively to their perspective. There might be underlying issues or misunderstandings that are contributing to their behavior.

Offer constructive feedback and possible solutions. This could include suggestions for leadership training, coaching, or changes in management practices. Clearly communicate your boundaries and expectations moving forward. It's important to articulate what changes you hope to see. After the conversation, monitor any changes in the leader's behavior. Follow up as necessary to reinforce the discussion and ensure that constructive steps are being taken. If the direct approach does not lead to positive changes, or if the destructive behavior continues, it may be necessary to escalate the issue to higher management or HR. This should be done professionally, with a focus on the well-being of the team and the organization. Dealing with destructive leaders requires courage, tact, and a commitment to the greater good of the team and organization. While it can be challenging, addressing these issues directly is often the first step in creating a more positive and productive work environment.

Transitioning to more constructive leadership styles is a nuanced process that hinges on self-awareness, education, and a dedication to ongoing improvement. Leaders looking to make this shift need to start with a comprehensive self-assessment, evaluating their current style and its impact. Tools such as 360-degree feedback, personality assessments, and reflective exercises can offer valuable insights into their behavior, highlighting both strengths and areas needing development.

Actively seeking feedback from colleagues, subordinates, and supervisors is critical. This feedback should be welcomed as an opportunity for growth, providing diverse perspectives on a leader's impact and effectiveness. Coupled with this, leaders should engage in leadership development programs and training focusing on key skills like emotional intelligence, communication, empathy, and ethical decision-making. Such education equips them with necessary tools for positive leadership.

Setting concrete goals for improvement based on self-assessment and feedback is a vital step. These goals should be specific and measurable, focusing on enhancing particular skills or altering certain behaviors. Practicing these new behaviors in day-to-day leadership roles is essential for embedding them into one's leadership style. Seeking mentorship from those who exemplify constructive leadership can also be incredibly beneficial. Observing and learning from these role models offers practical examples and insights into effective leadership practices. Alongside, building a network of supportive peers and colleagues can provide the necessary encouragement and accountability. This network is a resource for ongoing feedback, advice, and support.

Encouraging a culture of feedback within the organization is also crucial. This means not only receiving feedback but also giving constructive feedback to others, fostering an environment of continuous learning and development. Regularly reviewing progress towards leadership goals and remaining open to ongoing adjustments is key. Leadership development is not a one-time event but a continuous journey, with even small improvements having a significant impact over time.

Continuous reflection on the impact of one's leadership on the team's morale, productivity, and overall well-being reinforces the importance of maintaining and refining constructive leadership practices. Such reflection ensures that leaders remain mindful of their influence and committed to fostering a positive, supportive, and effective work environment.

Transitioning to a more constructive leadership style is a journey that requires commitment, self-awareness, and adaptability. It involves a holistic approach encompassing learning, practice, feedback, and continuous reflection, all aimed at fostering a leadership style that positively impacts both individuals and the organization. The journey from under the shadow of destructive leadership to a healthier, more effective leadership environment, as outlined in the chapters, is a transformative process that addresses the complexities and challenges of leadership in the modern organizational context.

Empowering employees to voice concerns and participate in creating solutions is a pivotal strategy in shifting away from toxic leadership. Equipping employees with the tools and confidence to express their thoughts and ideas contributes to a more open, inclusive, and dynamic workplace. Effective leadership is not just about driving business success; it's about fostering a positive work environment, promoting ethical practices, and supporting employee well-being. Leaders set the tone for the organization, and their commitment to positive values and behaviors is instrumental in cultivating a constructive culture.

Dealing with destructive leaders directly and transitioning to more constructive leadership styles are practical steps in this journey. This involves confronting toxic behaviors, setting clear expectations for change, and implementing strategies for developing more empathetic, transparent, and effective leadership practices.

The chapter also outlined processes and techniques for building a healthier leadership environment. This includes establishing organizational policies and practices that support open communication, employee well-being, and ethical behavior. The journey underscores the necessity of continuous learning, self-reflection, and adaptation for leaders to thrive and foster a healthy workplace culture.

In the ever-evolving landscape of modern business, being a successful leader requires more than just adhering to a fixed set of skills or behaviors. It demands an ongoing commitment to self-improvement, responsiveness to change, and an acute awareness of how one's leadership style impacts others and the organization as a whole. Continuous vigilance in leadership involves being perpetually alert to the dynamics of the team, the organization, and the broader industry. Leaders must be aware of the changing needs, challenges, and opportunities that arise and be prepared to adjust their strategies accordingly. This vigilance also means being attuned to the well-being and morale of their team, recognizing signs of stress or disengagement early, and taking steps to address them.

Adaptation is equally critical. The business world is characterized by rapid changes – technological advancements, shifting market demands, evolving customer expectations, and changing workforce dynamics. Leaders must be agile, ready to evolve their strategies and approaches to stay relevant and effective. This adaptability also applies to personal leadership styles; what works well in one situation or with one team may not be as effective in another context.

Continuous learning is a cornerstone of vigilant and adaptive leadership. This involves keeping abreast of new trends and developments in their field, as well as broader topics like leadership theories, emotional intelligence, and organizational behavior. Engaging in regular training, seeking feedback, and being open to new ideas and perspectives are essential for growth and adaptation. Leaders also play a key role in fostering a culture of learning and adaptability within their organizations. By encouraging innovation, supporting professional development, and demonstrating openness to change, leaders can create an environment where continuous improvement is valued and pursued by all.

The need for continuous vigilance and adaptation in leadership practices reflects the dynamic nature of business and the complex challenges faced by organizations today. Leaders who embrace this approach are better equipped to lead their teams effectively, drive organizational success, and navigate the challenges and opportunities of the ever-changing business environment.

Part II: "The Zen Masters: Militant Neutrality in Leadership"

"Balanced leadership is like a river flowing steadily; it nourishes all in its path."

"In the calmness of balance, great decisions are made."

"In balance, there is harmony."

- Anonymous Zen Wisdom -

Part II marks a pivotal transition from the dark side of leadership to a more balanced approach. Here, we explore the concept of Militant Neutrality, where leadership is neither overly aggressive nor passively inactive, but rather a harmonious blend of strength and empathy.

In "Walking the Tightrope: The Art of Balance," we delve into how leaders can maintain this delicate equilibrium, navigating through challenges while keeping their teams united and motivated. "The Empathetic Gladiator: Being Kind Yet Firm" explores the intricate dance of being compassionate without losing the authority necessary to lead effectively.

Through "Grey Stories: The Middle Path Successes," we bring to light real-world examples of leaders who have successfully walked this middle path, illustrating the profound impact of this balanced approach.

Finally, "Becoming a Zen Master: Practical Tips" provides readers with actionable advice and strategies to cultivate their own style of Militant Neutrality, encouraging leaders to become more adaptable, fair, and effective.

This part of the book is about finding harmony in leadership, steering clear of extremes, and embracing the power of balance to create a positive, productive, and inclusive environment.

Chapter 5: "Walking the Tightrope: The Art of Balance"

In this chapter, we explore the intricate world of balanced leadership, a vital skill for effective management and organizational success. Balanced leadership is about maintaining equilibrium between various, often competing, qualities and approaches. It involves a nuanced understanding of when to take charge and when to step back, when to be firm and when to be flexible, and how to harmoniously blend contrasting leadership styles to suit different situations. At the heart of balanced leadership is the concept of equilibrium. This is not about being moderate in all things; rather, it's about having the agility and awareness to shift your approach according to the needs of the moment. It requires an acute sensitivity to the dynamics of your team and the demands of the situation, and the ability to respond with the appropriate leadership style.

We explore why this balance is crucial. For one, it prevents the pitfalls of an overly authoritarian or excessively laissez-faire approach. It also fosters a more dynamic, responsive, and ultimately effective leadership style. By striking the right balance, leaders can inspire trust and respect, drive productivity, and create a positive work environment conducive to both individual and collective success.

In subsequent sections, we'll break down the key aspects of balanced leadership, offering practical strategies and real-world examples to illustrate how this approach can be effectively implemented in various organizational contexts. This exploration will not only enhance your understanding of what it takes to be a balanced leader but will also equip you with the tools to apply this concept in your own leadership journey.

Maintaining balance in leadership is a challenging endeavor, often riddled with pitfalls and obstacles. Leaders striving for equilibrium must navigate a landscape where missteps can easily tilt the scales too far in one direction. Here are some common challenges they face:

- Overcorrection: Leaders might overcompensate in one area to make up for a perceived lack in another. This could lead to extremes in behavior, such as being too authoritarian in an attempt to assert control or too lenient in an effort to be liked, ultimately disrupting the balance.

- Inconsistent Application: Balance in leadership requires consistency. A leader who vacillates between different styles can create confusion and uncertainty among team members. Inconsistency in decision-making or interpersonal interactions can undermine a leader's credibility and effectiveness.

- Stress and Burnout: The effort to maintain balance, especially in high-pressure environments, can be mentally and emotionally taxing. Leaders might experience stress or burnout, which can impair their judgment and ability to maintain a balanced perspective.

- Misreading Situations: Effective balanced leadership hinges on correctly reading situations and adapting accordingly. Misinterpreting team dynamics, organizational culture, or external factors can lead to inappropriate responses, upsetting the balance.

- Resistance to Change: Some leaders may find it challenging to adapt their style, particularly if they have been successful with a particular approach in the past. This resistance to change can hinder their ability to balance different leadership aspects as situations evolve.

- Lack of Self-awareness: A critical aspect of balanced leadership is self-awareness. Leaders who lack insight into their strengths and weaknesses may struggle to strike the right balance, as they may not recognize when and how to adjust their approach.

- External Pressures: Leaders often face pressures from stakeholders with varying expectations and demands. Balancing these diverse and sometimes conflicting external pressures while staying true to one's leadership style and organizational goals can be difficult.

Overcoming these challenges requires self-reflection, a willingness to adapt, and an understanding of the nuanced demands of leadership roles. Continuous learning, feedback from peers and team members, and a supportive environment can help leaders navigate these pitfalls and maintain a balanced approach. Maintaining balance in leadership can be challenging, as evidenced by real-world examples across various sectors:

In the corporate world, an authoritarian CEO making unilateral decisions may bring short-term efficiency but can stifle innovation and morale, leading to high staff turnover. Conversely, a startup founder with a laissez-faire approach might create a relaxed culture, but this can result in a lack of direction and chaos as the company grows. Political leadership during crises offers another perspective. A leader who remains rigid and refuses to adapt during a crisis can exacerbate the situation, as seen in historical instances of political leaders failing to respond effectively to economic or social upheavals.

In the educational sector, a school principal focusing solely on academic performance while neglecting emotional and social development can create an imbalanced environment. While academic scores might rise, this approach can increase student stress and hinder holistic development. Sports leadership provides a different angle. A coach who emphasizes physical training, but neglects athletes' psychological well-being might achieve short-term success. However, this can lead to athlete burnout, decreased performance, and a lack of team cohesion over time. Finally, in change management, a leader who concentrates on technical aspects like new systems or processes and overlooks the human element, such as employee concerns and morale, can face resistance, low adoption rates, and potentially fail in the change initiative.

These examples highlight the need for leaders to adapt their style to the context and the needs of their team or organization, underscoring the importance of a balanced approach in leadership.

Balanced decision-making is a key skill for effective leadership, involving the integration of multiple perspectives and a careful consideration of various factors. This involves actively seeking input from team members and stakeholders. By consulting with a diverse group, leaders can gather a range of viewpoints, which helps in making more informed, well-rounded decisions.

Leaders should not only rely on logical reasoning but also consider emotional aspects. Understanding and empathizing with how decisions impact the emotions and morale of the team can lead to more considerate and effective outcomes. Before making a decision, leaders can evaluate different scenarios. This means considering the potential outcomes of various choices, assessing risks and benefits, and anticipating possible challenges. Effective decision-making requires considering both immediate needs and long-term objectives. Leaders should weigh the immediate impact of their decisions against their alignment with long-term goals. After making decisions, seeking feedback on their effectiveness and reflecting on the outcomes can provide valuable insights. This process helps in honing decision-making skills and achieving a more balanced approach in the future.

The ability to adapt decisions in response to changing circumstances is crucial. This flexibility allows leaders to adjust their approach as new information becomes available or as situations evolve. Making use of data-driven insights can help in adding an objective layer to the decision-making process. Analyzing data can uncover trends and patterns that might not be obvious through subjective assessment alone. By incorporating these techniques, leaders can make decisions that are more balanced, taking into account a variety of needs, perspectives, and implications. This approach not only enhances the quality of the decisions but also contributes to a more inclusive and dynamic leadership style.

Balancing short-term needs with long-term goals is a crucial aspect of leadership and strategic planning. It involves navigating the often-competing demands of immediate requirements and future aspirations. Leaders face the challenge of addressing current issues like cash flow management, employee morale, or customer satisfaction, while also laying the groundwork for long-term objectives such as market expansion, innovation, and sustainable growth. The key is to not let the urgency of short-term issues overshadow the importance of long-term planning.

One effective approach is to align short-term actions with long-term goals. This means making decisions that solve immediate problems without derailing future plans. For instance, in a financial crunch, rather than making drastic cuts that could hinder long-term innovation, a leader might explore temporary measures that preserve the company's future growth potential. Another aspect is to maintain flexibility in both planning and execution. The business landscape is dynamic, and leaders must be prepared to adapt their strategies as new information and opportunities arise. This adaptability ensures that both short-term and long-term plans remain relevant and effective.

Effective communication is also key. Leaders should articulate how short-term actions fit into the larger picture, helping team members understand and stay committed to long-term objectives. This creates a shared vision and keeps everyone aligned towards common goals. Regular review and adjustment of both short-term and long-term plans are necessary. As situations evolve, leaders need to reassess their strategies to ensure they are still on track to achieving their long-term goals without neglecting immediate needs.

Balancing short-term needs with long-term goals requires strategic alignment, flexibility, effective communication, and ongoing reassessment. This balanced approach helps leaders steer their teams and organizations through the complexities of the present while preparing for the future. Emotional intelligence plays a pivotal role in achieving and maintaining balance in leadership. It involves the ability to understand and manage one's own emotions, as well as to recognize and influence the emotions of others. This skill set is crucial for leaders aiming to strike a balance in various aspects of their role.

Understanding one's own emotions is the first step. Leaders with high emotional intelligence are more self-aware. They recognize how their feelings can affect their decisions, interactions, and leadership style. This self-awareness allows them to regulate their responses, avoiding overreactions and maintaining a calm, balanced approach even in challenging situations. Recognizing the emotions of others is equally important. Leaders who can empathize with their team members are better equipped to understand their perspectives and needs. This understanding helps in tailoring communication, feedback, and support to suit individual team members, fostering a positive, inclusive, and motivating work environment.

Emotional intelligence also enhances a leader's ability to handle stress and conflict. By understanding and managing emotions, leaders can navigate tense situations more effectively, maintaining harmony and preventing escalation. This ability to manage conflict is crucial for maintaining balance within a team. In decision-making, emotional intelligence allows leaders to consider the emotional impact of their choices. This leads to decisions that are not only logical but also considerate of the team's morale and well-being, contributing to a balanced and supportive work culture.

Emotional intelligence is key in adapting leadership styles to suit different situations. A leader who can read a situation and understand the emotional undercurrents can adjust their approach accordingly. This flexibility is essential for maintaining balance, especially in dynamic and rapidly changing environments. Overall, emotional intelligence is a fundamental component of balanced leadership. It enhances self-awareness, empathy, stress management, conflict resolution, and adaptive decision-making, all of which are essential for leaders seeking to maintain a balanced and effective leadership approach.

Developing self-awareness and empathy is critical for effective leadership, as these qualities are foundational to understanding both oneself and others. Regular reflection on one's actions, decisions, and their outcomes can significantly boost self-awareness. This could involve journaling, meditation, or simply setting aside time for introspection. Actively seeking and openly receiving feedback from colleagues, mentors, and team members can provide insights into one's leadership style and areas for improvement. Utilizing psychological tests and self-assessment tools, like personality tests or 360-degree feedback, can help leaders gain a deeper understanding of their strengths, weaknesses, and behavioral tendencies. Participating in leadership workshops, coaching, or counseling can offer structured opportunities for self-discovery and growth. Practicing active listening, where the focus is entirely on the speaker and understanding their perspective, is a powerful way to develop empathy.

Learning to recognize and understand emotions in others is crucial. This might involve studying non-verbal cues, understanding the impact of tone and body language, and recognizing the emotional context of conversations. As well as exposing oneself to a variety of cultures, perspectives, and situations can broaden understanding and appreciation of different viewpoints, enhancing empathy. Regularly engaging in conversations where the primary goal is to understand the other person's point of view helps in cultivating an empathetic mindset. Putting oneself in others' shoes, whether through role-playing exercises or thought experiments, can provide valuable insights into others' experiences and challenges.

By developing self-awareness and empathy, leaders can better understand their own motivations and behaviors and connect with their team members more effectively. This leads to a more cohesive, supportive, and productive work environment.

Navigating conflicting interests and demands is a common challenge for leaders. It's crucial to thoroughly understand the different interests and positions involved. This means engaging in dialogues with all parties, asking questions to uncover underlying concerns, and actively listening to their viewpoints. Leaders need to assess the relative importance of each interest. This involves considering the impact on the organization's goals, values, and stakeholders. Decisions should be based on objective criteria rather than personal preferences or biases.

Often, conflicting interests have some common elements. Identifying these areas of agreement can provide a foundation for building a mutually acceptable solution. Keeping communication open and transparent helps maintain trust among all parties. Clearly explaining decisions, the reasons behind them, and how they align with organizational goals can mitigate feelings of being overlooked or undervalued. Sometimes, standard solutions won't work in situations with conflicting interests. Employing creative problem-solving techniques can lead to innovative solutions that address the concerns of all parties. In cases where conflicts are deep-seated or complex, involving a neutral third party to mediate can be helpful. A skilled mediator can facilitate discussions, help clarify issues, and assist in finding a resolution.

Cultivating an organizational culture that values respect and consideration for diverse viewpoints can preemptively mitigate conflicts. When team members feel respected, they are more likely to engage in constructive dialogue and less likely to hold onto rigid positions. By applying these techniques, leaders can effectively navigate situations with conflicting interests, leading to solutions that are balanced, fair, and aligned with organizational objectives.

A multinational corporation faced a dilemma between cutting costs and maintaining employee satisfaction. The leadership conducted extensive consultations with department heads to understand the impact of cost-cutting on various teams. They prioritized measures that saved costs without significant layoffs, such as reducing non-essential expenses and optimizing operations. They also initiated a program to increase operational efficiency, involving employees in the process. This approach not only achieved the necessary cost reductions but also maintained employee morale and engagement.

In another instance, a healthcare provider had to balance patient care with financial sustainability. The leadership team, including medical and administrative staff, collaborated to identify areas where costs could be reduced without compromising patient care. They adopted new technologies to streamline administrative processes and renegotiated supplier contracts. The savings were then reinvested into patient care services. This strategy successfully navigated the conflicting interests of financial health and patient care quality.

A technology startup faced conflicts between the development team's desire for innovation and the sales team's need for a stable, easy-to-sell product. The CEO organized joint workshops where both teams shared their perspectives and challenges. Through these sessions, a compromise was reached: the company would pursue incremental innovation, allowing the development team to explore new ideas while providing the sales team with a stable product to market. This approach fostered a culture of collaboration and mutual understanding.

These case studies demonstrate how effective leadership, involving open communication, collaboration, and creative problem-solving, can successfully navigate conflicting interests, leading to outcomes that satisfy multiple stakeholders and align with organizational goals.

Maintaining personal balance and well-being for leaders involves setting clear boundaries between work and personal life, engaging in regular self-care activities like exercise and hobbies, and practicing mindfulness and meditation for stress management.

Continuously learning and growing through reading, workshops, or pursuing hobbies provides fulfillment and balance.

Building a strong support network of friends, family, and professional contacts offers emotional backing, while seeking professional help like coaching or therapy can be beneficial in high-stress situations or complex issues. Additionally, regular medical check-ups are important for monitoring health. These practices, woven into a leader's routine, are essential for sustaining their effectiveness and resilience in professional roles.

A leader's personal balance significantly impacts their leadership style. When leaders maintain a good balance in their personal life, it reflects in their professional demeanor, leading to a more composed, empathetic, and effective leadership style. A well-balanced leader tends to have a clear mind, which is crucial for making sound decisions. They are less likely to make impulsive or emotionally charged decisions, leading to a more stable and consistent leadership approach.

Leaders who manage their stress well and maintain their well-being are more likely to foster a positive work environment. They can be more patient, better listeners, and more approachable, all of which arc qualities that inspire and motivate their team. This positivity often translates into higher team morale and productivity. Leaders who prioritize their well-being serve as role models for their team, demonstrating the importance of work-life balance. This can encourage a healthier work culture within the organization, where employees feel valued and are less likely to experience burnout.

In contrast, a leader struggling with personal imbalance may exhibit signs of stress, burnout, or inconsistency in their leadership style. This can lead to a negative work environment, poor decision-making, and strained team dynamics. Therefore, a leader's personal balance is not just beneficial for their own well-being but is also a critical component of effective and inspirational leadership.

Creating and nurturing an organizational culture that values and reflects balance is a multifaceted process. It starts with leadership demonstrating balance in their actions and decisions, setting a precedent for the entire organization. Implementing policies that promote work-life balance, like flexible working hours or remote work options, can significantly contribute to this culture. Encouraging regular breaks and vacations without a culture of guilt or fear of falling behind is also vital.

Training and development programs focused on stress management, time management, and emotional intelligence can equip employees with the tools to maintain their own balance. Open communication channels where employees feel heard, and their concerns are addressed can foster a supportive and inclusive environment. Recognizing and rewarding not just hard work but also smart work that promotes efficiency without burnout is crucial.

Regularly assessing and adjusting organizational practices to ensure they align with the goal of balance is necessary. This might involve surveys or feedback sessions with employees to understand their needs and experiences. Lastly, creating a sense of community within the workplace where employees feel connected and supported can enhance overall well-being and balance. This comprehensive approach ensures that the value of balance is deeply embedded in the organizational culture, benefiting both the employees and the organization as a whole.

The role of policies, training, and communication in fostering a culture of balance within an organization is crucial. Policies like flexible working hours, remote work options, and adequate leave entitlements provide a structural framework that supports work-life balance. These policies demonstrate an organizational commitment to the well-being of employees. Training programs are equally important. They can focus on skills like stress management, time management, and emotional intelligence, empowering employees to maintain their own balance and well-being.

Communication plays a pivotal role in this process. Open and transparent communication channels enable employees to express their needs and concerns. Regular meetings, surveys, and feedback mechanisms allow leaders to gauge employee satisfaction and address issues related to work-life balance. Communicating success stories and examples of balance within the organization can also inspire and encourage employees to prioritize their own well-being.

Consistent messaging from leadership about the importance of balance and well-being helps in reinforcing these values. Leaders who openly discuss and demonstrate their commitment to balance set a powerful example for the rest of the organization. By integrating supportive policies, targeted training, and effective communication, organizations can successfully foster a culture that values and reflects balance.

Emphasizing the ongoing nature of maintaining balance in leadership is crucial, as it is not a one-time achievement but a continuous process. Leaders need to constantly assess and readjust their approach to ensure they're meeting both their personal needs and those of their organization. This includes regularly reflecting on their leadership style, seeking feedback, and being open to change. Market trends, organizational needs, and personal circumstances evolve, requiring leaders to adapt their strategies for maintaining balance.

The dynamic nature of leadership roles, with varying challenges and responsibilities, necessitates a flexible approach to balance. Leaders must be proactive in identifying when certain aspects of their role or personal life are being neglected and take corrective action. They also need to stay attuned to the well-being of their team, adjusting their leadership approach to maintain a positive and productive work environment. This ongoing process involves learning from experiences, both successes and failures, and using these insights to refine one's approach to leadership. Continual learning and personal development are key aspects of maintaining balance. Leaders who recognize the perpetual nature of this process are more likely to succeed in sustaining a balanced and effective leadership style over the long term.

Encouraging leaders to persistently assess and adjust their approach is vital in the ever-evolving landscape of leadership. Constant vigilance and flexibility are key. Leaders should regularly evaluate the effectiveness of their strategies, staying open to learning and growth. This involves being receptive to feedback, both from within the organization and from external sources. Leaders should also keep an eye on changing industry trends, organizational dynamics, and team needs, adapting their approach as necessary.

Self-reflection is another important aspect. Leaders should take time to introspect on their leadership style, the impact of their decisions, and their personal well-being. This ongoing self-assessment helps in identifying areas for improvement and in making necessary adjustments to maintain effectiveness and balance. Innovation in leadership strategies is also crucial. The willingness to try new approaches, learn from the outcomes, and refine tactics accordingly is essential for staying relevant and effective in a rapidly changing world.

Leaders should foster resilience. The journey to maintaining balance is often challenging and requires perseverance. Resilience enables leaders to navigate setbacks and challenges while remaining committed to their personal and professional growth. A leader's journey is one of continuous assessment and adjustment. Staying vigilant, adaptable, and resilient are the hallmarks of effective leadership, ensuring not only the success of the leader but also the well-being and advancement of their team and organization.

Chapter 6: "The Empathetic Gladiator: Being Kind Yet Firm"

This chapter introduces the concept of the 'Empathetic Gladiator,' a leadership approach that masterfully balances empathy with firmness. At its core, this style embodies the ability to be kind and understanding, yet assertive and decisive when the situation demands. It's about recognizing and responding to the emotional needs of team members while also maintaining clear standards and expectations.

The Empathetic Gladiator is not a contradiction, but a harmonious blend of qualities often seen as opposites. It involves understanding the perspectives and feelings of others, showing compassion and support, and at the same time, not shying away from tough decisions or difficult conversations. This balance is crucial in today's diverse and dynamic work environments, where leaders must navigate a range of challenges and personalities.

In this chapter, we will explore the nuances of being an empathetic yet firm leader. We'll delve into strategies for showing genuine care and understanding for team members' experiences and viewpoints, while also upholding standards and accountability. The aim is to equip leaders with the skills to create a supportive, positive work environment without compromising on performance and results. The journey of the Empathetic Gladiator is about striking the right balance between kindness and assertiveness, ensuring that leadership is both compassionate and effective. This approach not only enhances team morale and productivity but also fosters a culture of respect and high performance.

Empathy allows leaders to see situations from the perspectives of their team members, fostering a deeper understanding of their challenges, motivations, and needs. This understanding is crucial for building strong, trusting relationships within the team. When leaders demonstrate empathy, they create a supportive work environment where team members feel valued and understood. This not only boosts morale but also encourages open communication. Team members are more likely to share their thoughts, concerns, and ideas in an environment where they feel their leader genuinely cares about their well-being.

Empathetic leaders are also better equipped to resolve conflicts and manage team dynamics effectively. By understanding the emotional undercurrents within the team, they can address issues in a way that acknowledges and respects everyone's feelings and perspectives. Furthermore, empathy contributes to stronger collaboration and teamwork. When team members feel understood and supported, they are more inclined to cooperate and work towards common goals. This leads to increased productivity and a more harmonious work environment.

Empathy is a key ingredient in building and maintaining strong, cohesive teams. It enables leaders to connect with their team members on a deeper level, creating a foundation of trust, open communication, and mutual respect that is essential for effective teamwork and organizational success.

Real-world examples of empathetic leadership can be found in various sectors, demonstrating the profound impact empathy can have on leadership effectiveness. In the corporate world, a CEO of a major technology company made headlines by significantly reducing his own salary to increase the minimum wage for his employees. This decision, driven by an understanding of his employees' financial struggles, not only boosted morale but also led to increased loyalty and productivity within the company.

In the healthcare sector, a hospital administrator who regularly spent time with both patients and staff, listening to their experiences and concerns, was able to implement changes that significantly improved patient care and staff working conditions. This empathetic approach led to higher patient satisfaction rates and a more motivated workforce. In education, a principal who prioritized creating a safe and supportive environment for both students and teachers managed to turn around a struggling school. By addressing the emotional and educational needs of the students and supporting teachers in their roles, the school saw improved academic performance and decreased behavioral issues.

A non-profit leader, working in disaster relief, showed empathy not only to those affected by disasters but also to her team, acknowledging the emotional toll of their work. She implemented support systems for staff, leading to more effective and sustained relief efforts. In sports, a coach who focused on understanding and supporting his athletes' mental health and well-being, as well as their physical training, led his team to victory in a major championship. His empathetic approach resulted in a team that was not only physically strong but also mentally resilient.

These examples illustrate how empathetic leadership can lead to tangible positive outcomes, including increased morale, productivity, and overall success in various fields. Empathetic leaders are able to foster a sense of community and loyalty, driving forward both their teams and their organizations.

Asserting authority without resorting to aggressive tactics involves a blend of clear communication, confidence, and respect. Leaders can establish their authority by setting clear expectations and guidelines, ensuring that everyone understands their roles and responsibilities. Consistency in enforcing these standards is key; it demonstrates fairness and reliability. Confidence in one's leadership abilities is essential. This doesn't mean being overbearing but rather having a calm and assured presence that instills trust and respect. Leaders should articulate their vision and decisions confidently, backing them up with rationale and open to constructive dialogue.

Active listening plays a significant role in non-aggressive authority. By genuinely listening to team members' inputs and concerns, leaders validate their opinions and foster a collaborative environment. This approach encourages mutual respect and reduces the need for aggressive enforcement of authority. Effective delegation also demonstrates authority. By entrusting responsibilities to team members, leaders show confidence in their team's abilities while maintaining oversight. This balance of trust and control reinforces the leader's authority in a positive way. Leading by example is perhaps the most effective way to assert authority. Leaders who embody the qualities and behaviors they expect from their team naturally command respect and authority, eliminating the need for aggressive tactics.

Maintaining respect and credibility as a leader involves several key practices. Demonstrating integrity is crucial; leaders should consistently act in an honest and ethical manner. This builds trust and respect among team members and stakeholders. Showing competence in their role is also important. Leaders should have a strong understanding of their field and stay informed about industry trends and best practices.

Good communication is essential. Clear, transparent, and consistent communication helps in building credibility and ensures that team members are well-informed and aligned with the organization's goals. Being accountable is another critical aspect. Leaders should take responsibility for their decisions and actions, including admitting mistakes and learning from them.

Empathy and understanding towards team members' needs and challenges foster respect. Leaders should actively listen to their team and show that they value their contributions. Making fair and impartial decisions also reinforces respect and credibility. Leaders should avoid favoritism and ensure that their decisions are based on objective criteria. Being approachable and available to the team encourages open communication and builds trust. Leaders who are seen as accessible and willing to engage with their team members on a regular basis are more likely to be respected and deemed credible.

Examining successful leaders who have mastered the balance of empathy and firmness reveals a diverse array of individuals across various fields. A renowned CEO in the tech industry is known for his empathetic approach towards employees, promoting a culture of inclusivity and support, while also making bold, decisive business decisions that have significantly advanced the company's market position.

In the realm of politics, a particular world leader has been praised for her ability to empathize with the public, often connecting on a personal level, yet displaying firmness in her policy decisions and international negotiations, earning global respect for her leadership style. A celebrated non-profit leader has demonstrated this balance by advocating passionately for humanitarian causes, showing deep empathy for those in need, while also navigating complex political and funding landscapes with assertiveness and strategic acumen.

In the sports world, a coach with multiple championship titles is revered for his unique ability to understand and motivate players individually, while maintaining strict discipline and high standards in training and during games, a testament to his balanced leadership approach. A principal of a top-performing school has achieved remarkable success by fostering a nurturing and understanding environment for students and teachers, coupled with a steadfast commitment to academic excellence and accountability.

These leaders, through their diverse approaches, illustrate how the balance of empathy and firmness can lead to respected and effective leadership. Their ability to connect with people on a personal level, while also maintaining clear vision and decisiveness, has been key to their success. From the experiences of leaders who have successfully balanced empathy with firmness, several key lessons emerge:

- Understanding and valuing the human element in leadership is crucial. These leaders show that recognizing the individual needs and concerns of team members can lead to a more motivated and committed workforce.

- Clear vision and decisiveness are essential. Successful leaders demonstrate the importance of having a strong direction and making firm decisions, even in the face of adversity, ensuring progress and stability.

- Communication is a powerful tool. These leaders exemplify the importance of clear, transparent communication in building trust and guiding teams effectively.

- Adaptability and flexibility are vital traits. The ability to adjust one's leadership style to suit different situations and challenges is a common thread among these leaders.

- Consistency in actions and values builds credibility. These leaders maintain their integrity and credibility by consistently acting in line with their values and principles.

- The importance of leading by example is evident. They show that embodying the qualities and behaviors expected from others is a powerful way to inspire and lead effectively.

- Continuous learning and self-reflection are key to leadership growth. These leaders highlight the importance of learning from experiences, both successes and failures, and using these insights to improve their leadership approach.

Effective communication that is both kind and assertive involves a blend of clarity, empathy, and confidence. Using clear and concise language helps in ensuring that the message is understood as intended, avoiding misunderstandings. Empathy plays a crucial role; communicating in a way that shows understanding and consideration for the receiver's feelings and perspective builds rapport and trust.

Active listening is essential in effective communication. It involves fully concentrating on the speaker, understanding their message, and responding thoughtfully. This not only shows respect but also provides a deeper understanding of the situation, leading to more effective responses. Non-verbal cues are important as well. Maintaining eye contact, using appropriate body language, and being mindful of tone and volume can reinforce the message and show assertiveness without aggression.

Being respectful and maintaining a positive tone, even when discussing difficult issues, is key. This approach can defuse tension and makes it easier for the other party to be receptive to the message. Focusing on the issue, not the person, helps in keeping discussions constructive. Framing feedback or criticism in terms of behaviors and impacts rather than personal attributes prevents defensiveness and facilitates a more productive dialogue. Finally, asserting oneself while also being open to other perspectives demonstrates confidence and respect for others' viewpoints. This balance encourages open and honest communication, fostering a collaborative and respectful environment.

Balancing listening with decisive action is crucial for effective leadership. It involves genuinely hearing and considering team members' input while retaining the ability to make timely and clear decisions. Active listening shows respect for others' opinions and ideas, which can lead to more informed and well-rounded decisions. It's important for leaders to create an environment where team members feel comfortable sharing their thoughts openly.

However, listening should be coupled with decisiveness. After gathering necessary information and perspectives, leaders need to analyze the input and make decisions confidently. Procrastination or indecision can be as harmful as hasty, uninformed decisions. Decisive action demonstrates leadership strength and provides clear direction to the team.

Leaders should also communicate their decisions effectively, explaining how they considered various inputs and why a particular course of action was chosen. This transparency helps in maintaining trust and respect, even among those who may have different viewpoints. Being open to adjusting decisions based on new information or feedback is a part of this balance. It shows that a leader values input and is committed to the best outcomes, not just to being right.

Balancing listening with decisive action involves valuing team input, making informed decisions promptly, communicating decisions transparently, and being adaptable to change. This balance fosters a respectful, collaborative, and effective leadership environment.

Empathetic yet firm leadership has a significant positive influence on team morale and productivity. Empathy from a leader creates a supportive and understanding work environment, where team members feel valued and respected. This boosts morale, as employees feel their personal and professional needs are recognized and addressed. Such an environment encourages open communication. Team members are more likely to share ideas, concerns, and feedback, contributing to a culture of trust and collaboration. This open dialogue often leads to innovative solutions and improvements in processes, enhancing productivity.

The firm aspect of this leadership style ensures that while empathy is prevalent, there is also a clear direction and expectation of performance. This balance keeps the team focused and driven, preventing complacency. Team members understand their roles, responsibilities, and the standards to which they are held, which clarifies objectives and streamlines efforts towards achieving them. This leadership style can lead to increased loyalty and lower turnover. Employees often feel more committed to leaders and organizations that show genuine concern for their well-being while also pushing them towards excellence. The sense of being part of a team that cares, but also demands high standards, can be very motivating.

Empathetic yet firm leadership also helps in managing conflicts effectively. By understanding different viewpoints and addressing issues with fairness and assertiveness, leaders can resolve disputes efficiently, minimizing disruptions and maintaining a positive work environment. Overall, empathetic yet firm leadership fosters a workplace where employees are motivated, engaged, and aligned with the organization's goals, leading to enhanced morale and productivity.

Building a culture of trust and respect in an organization involves several key practices. It starts with leaders demonstrating trustworthiness through consistent, honest, and transparent actions. Being reliable, following through on promises, and communicating openly about decisions and changes builds credibility and trust. Respect is fostered by valuing and acknowledging the contributions of all team members. Recognizing achievements, providing constructive feedback, and treating everyone with fairness and dignity reinforces a culture of respect.

Creating an inclusive environment where diverse opinions and backgrounds are valued and encouraged is essential. This means actively listening to different perspectives and fostering a sense of belonging for all employees. Empowering employees by entrusting them with responsibilities and giving them the autonomy to make decisions in their areas of expertise also builds trust. It shows confidence in their abilities and judgment. Providing support and resources for employee growth and development demonstrates a commitment to their professional and personal well-being. This not only helps in building trust but also encourages loyalty.

Encouraging open communication and providing safe channels for feedback and concerns allow employees to express themselves without fear of reprisal. This openness is key to maintaining a transparent and respectful culture. Handling conflicts fairly and promptly, showing empathy and understanding, and being approachable as a leader are also important in building a culture of trust and respect.

These practices, consistently applied, create an environment where trust and respect are integral to the organizational culture, leading to a more positive, productive, and harmonious workplace.

Making tough decisions while maintaining empathy and firmness requires a balanced approach. Leaders need to be clear and decisive, ensuring that their decisions are aligned with organizational goals and values. It's important to analyze the situation thoroughly, considering all possible outcomes and their impact on the team and the organization. Empathy comes into play by understanding and acknowledging how these decisions will affect team members. Communicating decisions with sensitivity and care, explaining the reasoning behind them, and being transparent about the factors that influenced the decision-making process are crucial.

Even when decisions are difficult, maintaining a respectful and considerate tone helps in mitigating negative reactions. It's important for leaders to listen to any concerns or feedback from their team regarding the decision, showing that they value their input and perspective. Being available to provide support and guidance in the aftermath of tough decisions is also key. This may involve offering additional resources, training, or simply being there to address any uncertainties or challenges that arise.

While empathy is important, it's essential for leaders to stand firm on their decisions once made, especially if they are critical for the business's success or necessary for resolving significant issues. This firmness demonstrates commitment and confidence in the direction chosen. Reflecting on the outcomes of tough decisions, learning from them, and being open to making adjustments in the future, if necessary, are all part of balancing empathy and firmness in leadership.

A tech company faced financial challenges and had to downsize. The CEO, known for a compassionate leadership style, approached this difficult decision with transparency. She communicated the reasons for the layoffs clearly, expressing genuine regret. The company provided generous severance packages, career counseling, and job placement assistance. Despite the tough decision, the CEO's empathetic approach maintained employee trust and company reputation.

In the healthcare sector, a hospital administrator needed to implement budget cuts. Understanding the impact on staff and patient care, she involved department heads in the decision-making process. Together, they identified areas to reduce costs without compromising patient care. The administrator's firm decision-making, combined with her empathetic inclusion of staff in the process, led to effective cost-cutting with minimal negative impact.

A school principal faced the challenge of implementing a new, more rigorous curriculum. Knowing this would increase workload for teachers and students, she held meetings to address concerns and gather input. She provided additional resources and support to ease the transition. Her firm stance on the curriculum change, coupled with her empathetic listening and support, facilitated a smooth implementation.

In a retail company, a manager had to enforce a new policy that was unpopular with the staff. She held a team meeting to explain the reasons behind the policy and how it would benefit the company in the long run. She acknowledged the team's concerns and assured them of her support in adapting to the change. Her empathetic yet firm approach helped the team accept and adapt to the new policy.

These cases illustrate how leaders can navigate difficult decisions with a balance of empathy and firmness. By communicating openly, involving others in the process, and providing support, leaders can maintain trust and respect even in challenging situations.

The empathetic yet firm leadership style holds significant importance and impact in the realm of effective management and team dynamics. This style enables leaders to connect with their team on a deeper level, fostering a supportive and understanding work environment while maintaining clear expectations and a strong direction. Such leaders are adept at building trust and loyalty, as their empathy demonstrates care for their team's well-being and perspectives, while their firmness ensures that organizational goals and standards are met.

This balanced approach enhances team morale and motivation. Employees feel valued and heard, which boosts their engagement and willingness to contribute. At the same time, the firm aspect of this leadership style provides the necessary guidance and structure, leading to increased productivity and efficiency.

Conflict resolution is another area where this leadership style proves effective. The empathetic yet firm leader can navigate disputes with a keen understanding of different viewpoints, making fair and respected decisions. This ability to manage conflicts while maintaining respect and consideration for all parties involved is crucial for a harmonious work environment. This leadership style is adaptable to various situations, making it a versatile approach in the ever-changing landscape of business and organizational challenges. It allows leaders to be responsive and flexible, adjusting their approach to meet the needs of different scenarios while maintaining a consistent core of empathy and assertiveness.

The empathetic yet firm leadership style is integral for creating a positive, productive, and respectful work culture. It balances human understanding with decisive action, leading to a well-rounded and effective leadership approach. The journey towards mastering the balance between empathy and firmness in leadership is an ongoing process, demanding continuous self-reflection and improvement. Leaders should embrace regular self-evaluation and actively seek feedback to understand their effectiveness in this delicate balance. Professional development, through workshops, training, and staying abreast of current leadership trends, plays a crucial role in honing these skills. Cultivating self-awareness is fundamental, as it helps leaders understand their emotional drivers and manage their responses more effectively. Developing empathy, a cornerstone of this leadership style, involves deeply listening to and genuinely understanding the perspectives of team members. Leaders must also remain flexible, adapting their approach to suit varying situations and team needs.

Building and nurturing a support network of peers and mentors provides invaluable insights and encouragement. Sharing experiences and challenges with fellow leaders can offer new perspectives and strategies, aiding in personal and professional growth. By committing to these practices, leaders can continuously refine their ability to balance empathy with firmness. This balance is not only key to effective leadership but also to fostering a positive, productive, and respectful work environment. It's a journey well worth undertaking for any leader dedicated to personal excellence and the success of their team and organization.

Chapter 7: "Grey Stories: The Middle Path Successes"

In this chapter, we explore the concept of Middle Path Leadership, an approach that skillfully navigates between the extremes often encountered in traditional leadership styles. This leadership paradigm emphasizes balance, blending various aspects of leadership to achieve a harmonious and effective management style.

Middle Path Leadership is rooted in the understanding that leadership is not black and white, but rather a spectrum of behaviors, strategies, and attitudes. It acknowledges that different situations and team dynamics call for different approaches. This style avoids the pitfalls of extreme approaches, such as being too authoritative or too lenient, too hands-on or too hands-off, and instead finds a balanced, moderate path that adapts to the needs of the moment.

The essence of Middle Path Leadership lies in its flexibility and adaptability. It involves assessing each situation on its own merits and responding with a leadership style that is neither too rigid nor too permissive. This approach recognizes the value in various leadership philosophies and integrates them to create a more nuanced, responsive, and effective style.

This chapter delves into the principles of Middle Path Leadership, illustrating how this approach can lead to successful outcomes in a range of scenarios. By exploring real-world examples and practical strategies, we will see how Middle Path Leadership can enhance decision-making, team dynamics, and overall organizational success. It's a journey through the 'grey areas' of leadership, where success often lies in the balance.

Leaders who have successfully navigated the Middle Path in their leadership styles come from various sectors, each demonstrating the effectiveness of this balanced approach.

In the technology sector, a CEO is renowned for her ability to blend visionary thinking with practical execution. She strikes a balance between encouraging innovative ideas and ensuring their feasible implementation, leading her company to pioneering achievements without losing sight of current market realities.

In the non-profit world, a director has skillfully balanced advocacy and pragmatism. While passionately fighting for their cause, they also engage in realistic negotiations and partnerships with different stakeholders, achieving significant advancements without compromising their core values.

A mayor of a large city exemplifies Middle Path Leadership in the political arena. They have managed to bridge the gap between progressive policies and conservative fiscal management, implementing socially impactful initiatives while maintaining economic stability.

In the education sector, a school principal has achieved remarkable success by combining a nurturing, student-centered approach with a strong emphasis on academic excellence. This balance has created an environment where students thrive both personally and academically.

In healthcare, a hospital administrator navigated the challenges of patient care and operational efficiency. By valuing both the quality of patient care and the need for efficient administrative processes, they improved patient satisfaction while also enhancing the hospital's operational effectiveness.

These leaders showcase the power of Middle Path Leadership. Their ability to avoid extremes, adapting their approach to the unique demands of their fields, has led to sustainable success and positive impacts in their respective areas.

The strategies and approaches of leaders who successfully navigate the Middle Path in leadership reveal a nuanced understanding of balance and adaptability.

- Integrating Vision with Practicality: The tech CEO's success lies in her ability to dream big while keeping her feet firmly on the ground. She encourages innovation but pairs it with rigorous feasibility analysis, ensuring that visionary ideas are grounded in practical reality.

- Balancing Advocacy with Pragmatism: The non-profit director's approach combines a strong commitment to their cause with a realistic understanding of what can be achieved. They leverage collaborations and negotiations to create win-win situations, advancing their mission while remaining adaptable to the realities of the sector.

- Merging Progressive and Conservative Approaches: The mayor's political success is attributed to their ability to find a middle ground between progressive initiatives and conservative management. This involves careful planning, stakeholder consultation, and a keen understanding of the socioeconomic landscape.

- Combining Nurturing with Academic Rigor: The school principal's strategy focuses on creating a supportive, student-centered environment while maintaining high academic standards. This balance is achieved through a curriculum that supports personal development alongside academic excellence, and a teaching approach that is both compassionate and challenging.

- Valuing Patient Care and Operational Efficiency: The hospital administrator's effectiveness comes from prioritizing patient care without neglecting operational efficiency. They implement policies and processes that enhance patient experiences while streamlining hospital operations, ensuring high-quality care in a sustainable, efficient system.

These strategies showcase how leaders can successfully navigate the Middle Path by being flexible and adaptable, integrating diverse aspects of leadership to suit the specific needs of their organizations and the people they serve. Their success underscores the importance of a balanced, holistic approach to leadership.

Discussing the unique challenges faced by leaders across various industries who practice Middle Path Leadership reveals a spectrum of complexities and demands specific to each sector.

In the technology industry, the startup CEO faces the challenge of driving innovation in a highly competitive and rapidly evolving market while ensuring the company remains stable and customer-focused. Balancing cutting-edge development with practical business applications is a constant juggling act.

The hospital CEO in healthcare deals with the intricate balance of providing top-quality patient care with the constraints of budget and operational efficiency. Navigating these conflicting demands, especially in an environment where patient outcomes are critical, presents a significant challenge.

For the university dean, the challenge lies in fostering academic excellence and intellectual rigor while also creating an inclusive environment that supports student well-being and personal development. Striking this balance in an educational setting involves aligning faculty, curriculum, and student services to these dual objectives.

In manufacturing, the plant manager contends with maximizing production efficiency and meeting market demands while ensuring worker safety and maintaining high morale. Balancing the pressures of production targets with the human element of the workforce is a complex task.

The bank executive in finance faces the challenge of innovating in financial products and pursuing market expansion while adhering to stringent risk management and regulatory compliance.

Balancing growth ambitions with the need for financial prudence and stability is a delicate endeavor.

In the non-profit sector, particularly in environmental advocacy, the leader faces the challenge of pushing for significant environmental change while working within the realms of political, social, and economic feasibility. Striking a balance between idealism and practicality in pursuit of sustainable environmental solutions is a unique challenge.

These leaders' challenges illustrate the complexity of applying Middle Path Leadership across different industries, each requiring a tailored approach to balance industry-specific demands with broader organizational and stakeholder needs.

Overall, Middle Path Leadership positively impacts organizational culture by fostering environments that value flexibility, innovation, and stability. This approach leads to improved performance, employee satisfaction, customer loyalty, and overall organizational success. Middle Path Leadership has a profound positive effect on organizations, enhancing various aspects of their function and culture. This leadership style leads to increased employee engagement and satisfaction. Leaders who balance firmness with empathy create an environment where employees feel valued and understood, boosting morale and reducing turnover.

In terms of decision-making, Middle Path Leadership fosters a more inclusive and well-rounded process. Leaders who consider multiple perspectives and avoid extremes are likely to make more informed and effective decisions, benefiting the organization as a whole. Organizational adaptability is another positive outcome. Middle Path Leaders, with their flexible and balanced approach, are better equipped to navigate changing market conditions and emerging challenges, ensuring the organization remains resilient and competitive.

In terms of innovation, this leadership style encourages a culture of creative thinking balanced with practical execution. This approach not only sparks innovative ideas but also ensures they are viable and aligned with the organization's goals. Conflict resolution within organizations also improves under Middle Path Leadership. Leaders adept at understanding various viewpoints and finding common ground can resolve disputes effectively, maintaining harmony and productivity. Middle Path Leadership enhances the organization's reputation. Balanced and effective leadership contributes to a positive public image, attracting customers, partners, and talent.

Middle Path Leadership positively impacts organizations by creating a supportive and dynamic work environment, making sound decisions, fostering adaptability and innovation, effectively managing conflicts, and enhancing the organization's overall reputation and success.

Several case studies across industries demonstrate the positive impacts of Middle Path Leadership:

In a global technology company, the CEO's balanced approach to innovation and market stability led to the successful launch of new products while maintaining a strong customer base. This strategy not only resulted in increased market share but also established the company as a leader in innovation and reliability.

A healthcare system under a Middle Path Leader significantly improved patient care while maintaining operational efficiency. By balancing the introduction of advanced medical technologies with streamlined administrative processes, the hospital achieved high patient satisfaction scores and improved financial performance.

An educational institution led by a Middle Path Principal saw remarkable improvements in both student well-being and academic performance. The balanced focus on emotional support and academic rigor resulted in higher graduation rates, improved mental health among students, and enhanced the institution's reputation.

In the manufacturing sector, a company led by a Middle Path Manager successfully implemented new production technologies while enhancing worker safety and satisfaction. This approach led to increased productivity, a decrease in workplace accidents, and a more motivated workforce, contributing to the company's industry-leading position.

A financial services firm under Middle Path Leadership navigated a period of economic uncertainty by balancing innovative financial products with risk management. This strategy not only protected the firm during a volatile period but also positioned it for growth as market conditions improved.

In the non-profit sector, an environmental organization achieved significant policy influence and community impact by balancing advocacy with practical environmental solutions. The leader's ability to work collaboratively with diverse stakeholders led to successful environmental initiatives and increased funding and support for the organization.

These case studies illustrate how Middle Path Leadership can positively impact organizations, leading to innovation, operational efficiency, improved employee and customer satisfaction, and overall organizational success.

For aspiring Middle Path leaders, key takeaways and lessons from these case studies include the importance of flexibility and adaptability. Effective leaders must be able to adjust their strategies and approaches in response to changing circumstances, balancing various aspects of leadership to suit different situations. Emphasizing the value of empathy alongside assertiveness is crucial. Understanding and addressing the needs and concerns of team members, while maintaining clear expectations and goals, fosters a positive and productive work environment.

In decision-making, incorporating diverse perspectives and avoiding extremes leads to more balanced and effective outcomes. Middle Path leaders should strive to consider all angles and implications of their decisions, ensuring they are well-informed and comprehensive. Building a culture of open communication and inclusivity is essential. Encouraging dialogue, feedback, and collaboration within the organization promotes a sense of belonging and respect, enhancing team cohesion and morale. Resilience and perseverance are key traits of successful Middle Path leaders. Navigating the middle path often involves facing resistance and finding a compromise between conflicting viewpoints or interests. Staying committed and resilient in the face of these challenges is vital for long-term success. Continuous learning and self-improvement are vital. Middle Path leaders should be committed to personal growth, seeking out new knowledge and skills to enhance their leadership capabilities and keep up with evolving industry trends and challenges.

These key takeaways underscore the dynamic and nuanced nature of Middle Path Leadership, offering valuable insights for aspiring leaders seeking to adopt this effective and balanced approach. Implementing Middle Path Leadership principles across various leadership contexts involves several strategies:

1. Adaptability is crucial. Leaders should assess each situation individually and determine the most appropriate response, rather than relying on a one-size-fits-all approach. This requires a deep understanding of the unique dynamics of each scenario.

2. Practicing active listening and empathy is essential. Leaders should make a conscious effort to understand the perspectives and concerns of their team members. This helps in making decisions that are considerate of different viewpoints and fosters a collaborative environment.

3. Maintaining clear communication is key. Leaders should articulate their vision and expectations clearly while being open to feedback and dialogue. This transparency helps in aligning the team with organizational goals and facilitates mutual understanding.

4. Balancing assertiveness with understanding is important. Leaders need to be firm in their decisions and direction while also being approachable and supportive. This balance helps in building respect and trust among team members.

5. Cultivating resilience and emotional intelligence aids in navigating the complexities of leadership. Leaders should be prepared to handle resistance and conflict, managing their own emotions and those of others effectively.

6. Implementing a culture of continuous learning and improvement can foster a more dynamic and adaptable leadership style. Encouraging personal and professional development among team members, as well as oneself, keeps the organization evolving and responsive to change.

By adopting these strategies, leaders can effectively implement Middle Path Leadership principles, adapting their approach to suit different contexts and challenges, and leading their teams to success.

The chapter on Middle Path Leadership encapsulates the transformative potential of this balanced approach in various leadership contexts. Emphasizing the significance of adaptability, it showcases how leaders can navigate complex scenarios by adjusting their strategies to suit specific situations and challenges. The approach underscores the importance of blending empathy with assertiveness, ensuring leaders are compassionate and understanding while also being decisive and goal-oriented. The chapter highlights the key role of effective communication in Middle Path Leadership. Clear, open communication not only aligns teams with organizational goals but also fosters a culture of inclusivity and mutual understanding. This approach promotes a collaborative environment, encouraging diverse viewpoints and fostering a sense of belonging among team members.

Middle Path Leadership is characterized by its dynamic nature, requiring leaders to be resilient and emotionally intelligent. The ability to handle resistance and conflict with a balanced, empathetic approach is a crucial aspect of this leadership style. Furthermore, the emphasis on continuous learning and self-improvement illustrates the importance of evolving and adapting as a leader.

The transformative potential of Middle Path Leadership lies in its ability to create a harmonious, productive, and positive work environment. By avoiding extremes and finding a balanced path, leaders can effectively navigate the complexities of their roles, driving organizational success and fostering a culture of respect, collaboration, and continuous growth. This chapter demonstrates that Middle Path Leadership is not just a strategy but a holistic approach to effective leadership and organizational excellence.

As we conclude this chapter on Middle Path Leadership, we encourage leaders to explore and embrace this approach. The journey towards becoming a Middle Path Leader is one of self-discovery, adaptability, and continuous growth. Leaders are urged to step beyond traditional leadership paradigms and consider the nuanced balance this style offers.

Incorporating Middle Path Leadership into your approach involves understanding the unique needs of your team and organization and responding with a balanced strategy that combines empathy, flexibility, and firmness. It's about navigating the fine line between different leadership extremes to find the most effective path forward.

Embracing this approach also means committing to personal and professional development. Leaders should seek out opportunities to learn and grow, expanding their understanding of various leadership styles and how they can be integrated into a cohesive, effective approach. Middle Path Leadership is about fostering an environment of open communication, mutual respect, and inclusivity. Leaders should strive to create a culture where diverse perspectives are valued and where team members feel supported and motivated. We encourage leaders to view Middle Path Leadership not just as a set of strategies, but as a mindset. It's an ongoing process of balancing various aspects of leadership to meet the evolving challenges and opportunities of today's dynamic world.

By exploring and embracing Middle Path Leadership, you can transform not only your approach to leadership but also the overall culture and performance of your organization. This journey, though challenging, is immensely rewarding and holds the key to sustainable success and fulfillment in your leadership role.

Chapter 8: "Becoming a Zen Master: Practical Tips"

In this chapter, we delve into the concept of Zen Mastery in the realm of leadership. Becoming a Zen Master in leadership is about cultivating a deep sense of balance, inner peace, and clarity in one's approach to managing teams and navigating organizational challenges. It's a journey towards mastering the art of serene leadership amidst the often chaotic and high-pressure business environment.

Zen Mastery in leadership is not just a metaphorical concept but a practical approach that emphasizes mindfulness, emotional intelligence, and a centered presence. It involves developing an acute awareness of one's mental and emotional states and using this awareness to lead with calmness, compassion, and insight. This style of leadership is marked by a focus on being fully present in the moment, maintaining a clear and uncluttered mind, and approaching challenges with a sense of calm and poise.

The importance of balance in this context refers to the ability to navigate between the extremes of any situation, maintaining equilibrium amidst various pressures and demands. Inner peace in leadership translates to a state of mental and emotional stability, which allows for clear thinking and effective decision-making. Clarity is about having a focused and undistracted mind, enabling a leader to see through complexities and make decisions that are aligned with the organization's values and goals.

This chapter will provide practical tips and strategies for cultivating Zen Mastery in your leadership practice. From mindfulness techniques to effective stress management and emotional regulation, we'll explore how leaders can develop the qualities of a Zen Master to enhance their leadership effectiveness and create a more harmonious and productive work environment.

To understand your personal leadership style, self-reflection exercises are invaluable tools. They help you gain insights into your strengths, weaknesses, and areas for improvement. Here are some practical exercises to facilitate this understanding.

Self-Reflection Exercises

1. Reflective Journaling: Regularly journaling about your leadership experiences can provide deep insights. Write about challenging situations, decisions you made, and their outcomes. Reflect on what you did well and areas where you could improve.

2. Feedback Analysis: Actively seek feedback from your team, peers, and supervisors. After receiving feedback, spend time analyzing it. Look for patterns in what others say about your leadership style.

3. Meditative Reflection: Set aside time for quiet, meditative reflection. Focus on your recent leadership experiences and ponder your emotional and mental responses to these situations. Meditation can help clear your mind, making it easier to gain deeper insights.

4. Role Model Reflection: Think about leaders you admire and why. Reflect on how these role models have influenced your leadership style and how you might further incorporate aspects of their style into your own.

5. Personality and Leadership Assessments: Engage in formal assessments like Myers-Briggs Type Indicator (MBTI) or the Leadership Practices Inventory (LPI). Analyzing the results can offer a structured understanding of your leadership style.

6. Critical Incident Reflections: Identify a few critical incidents in your leadership journey. Reflect on your actions, decisions, and their impacts. Consider alternative approaches and what you learned from these experiences.

7. Goal Alignment: Reflect on your personal goals and values and how they align with your leadership approach. This can help ensure that your leadership style is authentic and true to your core values.

8. Visualization Techniques: Visualize yourself in a leadership scenario. Imagine handling a challenging situation and reflect on how you would ideally respond. Visualization can help you prepare for future scenarios and identify areas where you need to develop.

9. Professional Coaching: Engaging with a professional coach can provide guided reflection. Coaches can ask probing questions that encourage deeper thinking about your leadership style.

10. Peer Discussion Groups: Participate in or form a discussion group with fellow leaders. Share experiences and insights. Hearing about others' leadership styles can offer fresh perspectives on your own.

These self-reflection exercises can significantly enhance your understanding of your personal leadership style, helping you to identify both your strengths and the areas where you can grow and improve.

Increasing self-awareness and mindfulness is essential for effective leadership. These techniques help you become more attuned to your thoughts, feelings, and actions, enabling you to lead with greater clarity and empathy. Here are some techniques to enhance self-awareness and mindfulness.

Self-Awareness and Mindfulness Techniques

1. Mindful Meditation: Regularly practice mindful meditation. Focus on your breath and observe your thoughts and feelings without judgment. This practice helps in developing a deeper awareness of your internal state.

2. Emotional Journaling: Keep a journal to record your emotions and reactions to daily events. This can help you identify patterns in your emotional responses and triggers, increasing self-understanding.

3. Active Listening: Practice active listening in your interactions. Focus fully on the speaker, observe their non-verbal cues, and withhold judgment or internal commentary. This enhances your ability to be present and attentive.

4. Body Scan Meditation: Engage in body scan meditation where you focus on each part of your body in turn, observing any sensations or tensions. This practice increases awareness of the mind-body connection.

5. Mindfulness Exercises: Incorporate short mindfulness exercises throughout your day. This could be as simple as pausing to fully experience a routine activity like drinking a cup of coffee or walking.

6. Feedback Solicitation: Regularly ask for feedback from colleagues, friends, and family. Be open to receiving this feedback as a tool for understanding how others perceive you and your actions.

7. Mindful Breathing: Whenever you feel stressed or overwhelmed, practice mindful breathing. Focus solely on your breath, allowing your mind to settle and gain clarity.

8. Yoga: Yoga combines physical postures, breathing exercises, and meditation. It enhances body awareness, control, and mental focus.

9. Guided Imagery: Use guided imagery exercises to visualize peaceful scenes or successful outcomes to challenging situations. This technique helps in calming the mind and focusing on positive outcomes.

10. Self-Reflection Retreats: Occasionally engage in self-reflection retreats or workshops. These can provide a structured environment for deep self-exploration and mindfulness practice.

By regularly practicing these techniques, you can enhance your self-awareness and mindfulness, leading to more thoughtful, balanced, and effective leadership.

Enhancing emotional intelligence, crucial for understanding and managing emotions in oneself and others, involves a multifaceted approach. Cultivate a deep understanding of your own emotions by regularly reflecting on your feelings and reactions. This can involve practices like journaling or mindfulness meditation, which help you become more aware of your emotional responses and triggers. Once you are aware of your emotions, work on managing them effectively. Techniques like deep breathing, pausing before reacting, and positive self-talk can be helpful. This also involves setting clear boundaries and understanding how to maintain your composure in challenging situations.

Try to understand and share the feelings of others. This involves active listening, being fully present in conversations, and putting yourself in others' shoes. Empathy strengthens your ability to connect with others on an emotional level. Focus on enhancing communication, teamwork, and conflict resolution skills. Effective emotional intelligence in leadership is often demonstrated through the ability to navigate social complexities and build strong relationships. Regularly ask for feedback on your emotional intelligence from colleagues, friends, or a coach. Their perspectives can provide insights into areas where you may need improvement.

Engage in emotional intelligence training. Participate in workshops or courses that focus on developing emotional intelligence. These can provide valuable tools and strategies for enhancing your ability to understand and manage emotions. View every interaction as an opportunity to practice and improve your emotional intelligence. Reflect on what went well and what could be improved after each experience. Believe in your ability to develop and enhance your emotional intelligence over time. This mindset encourages continuous learning and adaptation. Surround yourself with emotionally intelligent people. Their behavior can serve as a model for your own development. And importantly, stay informed. Read books, articles, and research on emotional intelligence to keep up with the latest theories and practices.

Training in active listening and clear, compassionate communication is crucial for effective leadership and interpersonal relationships. Here are some strategies to develop these skills.

Active Listening Training

- Attend workshops or seminars focused on active listening. These often include exercises that enhance your ability to listen attentively and understand messages more effectively.

- Practice reflective listening in everyday conversations, where you paraphrase what the speaker has said to confirm your understanding.

- Engage in exercises that focus on non-verbal cues, such as maintaining eye contact and observing body language, to improve your overall listening skills.

Clear Communication Training

- Enroll in communication skills courses that emphasize clarity and brevity in conveying messages.

- Practice writing and speaking exercises where you focus on getting your point across in a concise and straightforward manner.

- Learn techniques for structuring your communication effectively, whether it's in writing or speaking.

Compassionate Communication Training

- Explore training in empathy and emotional intelligence, which are foundational for compassionate communication.

- Practice exercises that involve understanding the emotions and perspectives of others, such as role-playing scenarios.

- Learn about non-violent communication, a technique developed by Marshall Rosenberg, which focuses on empathetic listening and expressing your needs without blame or judgment.

Combined Training:

- Participate in interactive workshops or role-playing sessions that combine active listening with clear and compassionate communication. These often simulate real-life scenarios for you to practice and receive feedback.

- Seek mentorship or coaching from individuals skilled in these areas. They can provide personalized guidance and feedback.

- Regularly engage in self-reflection about your communication and listening habits, identifying areas for improvement and noting progress.

By undergoing training in these areas and practicing regularly, you can significantly enhance your communication skills, leading to more effective, empathetic, and productive interactions both in your professional and personal life.

Handling difficult conversations with poise is an essential skill for effective leadership and requires a thoughtful approach. Start by preparing mentally and emotionally for the conversation. Acknowledge your feelings about the topic and consider the perspective of the other person. This preparation helps in approaching the conversation with a clear and calm mindset.

Establish a conducive environment for the conversation. Choose a private and neutral setting where both parties can speak without interruptions.

Begin the conversation with a positive intent. Clearly state your objective for the discussion and express your desire for a constructive outcome. Listen actively and empathetically. Give the other person time to express their views and feelings. Show that you are listening and that you value their perspective. Communicate clearly and assertively. Use 'I' statements to express your feelings and needs without placing blame. Be honest and direct in your communication.

Stay focused on the issue at hand. Avoid bringing up unrelated issues or past grievances. Keep the conversation on topic to find a resolution. Manage your emotions. If you feel the conversation is becoming too heated, take a deep breath, pause, or suggest taking a break and reconvening later. Seek to understand before being understood. Make an effort to understand the other person's viewpoint and concerns before presenting your own. Look for common ground and mutual understanding. Even in disagreement, there is often some shared agreement or understanding that can be built upon. End the conversation with a clear plan or resolution. Summarize what has been agreed upon and discuss the next steps.

Practicing firmness while maintaining empathy involves a delicate balance. Here are some practical exercises to develop this skill.

1. Role-playing: Engage in role-playing exercises where you act out scenarios that require both firmness and empathy. Switch roles to understand different perspectives.

2. Reflective Journaling: After interactions where you needed to be firm, journal about the experience. Reflect on how you maintained empathy while being assertive.

3. Feedback Gathering: After meetings or conversations where firmness was required, ask for feedback from a trusted

colleague or mentor on how well you balanced firmness with empathy.

4. Empathy Mapping: Create empathy maps for individuals you interact with. This involves considering their feelings, thoughts, and motivations, which helps in maintaining empathy when you need to be firm.

5. Assertive Communication Practice: In a controlled setting, practice assertive communication techniques. Focus on expressing your thoughts and needs clearly and respectfully.

6. Boundary Setting Exercises: Practice setting and communicating boundaries in personal and professional settings. Reflect on how to do this empathetically.

7. Mindfulness Meditation: Regularly practice mindfulness meditation focusing on empathy. This helps in developing a deeper understanding of others' feelings and perspectives.

8. Scenario Analysis: Write down challenging scenarios and outline how you would handle them with both firmness and empathy. Analyze different approaches and their potential outcomes.

9. Active Listening Drills: Engage in exercises that enhance active listening, such as summarizing what the other person has said before you respond. This practice helps in showing empathy.

10. Positive Affirmation: Develop affirmations that reinforce your ability to be both firm and empathetic. Regularly recite these to build your confidence in balancing these traits.

Role-playing scenarios provide valuable practice in handling various leadership challenges with empathy and firmness. These scenarios can be followed by real-life applications for reinforcement.

Scenario 1: Performance Review

Role-play a performance review with an underperforming employee. Practice delivering constructive feedback firmly while showing understanding for any challenges they face.

Real-life Application: Apply these skills in actual performance reviews, ensuring you address performance issues with clarity and compassion.

Scenario 2: Conflict Resolution

Simulate a conflict between two team members. Act as the mediator to resolve the conflict, balancing assertiveness in finding a solution while empathizing with both parties' viewpoints.

Real-life Application: Use these techniques when mediating actual workplace conflicts, ensuring a fair and empathetic resolution.

Scenario 3: Policy Enforcement

Role-play a situation where you need to enforce a new, unpopular policy. Communicate the policy firmly while empathizing with the team's concerns.

Real-life Application: Implement new policies in your workplace by clearly explaining the reasons and listening to any concerns from your team.

Scenario 4: Change Management

Simulate a scenario where you must lead a team through a major organizational change. Address their fears and resistance with understanding, while firmly guiding them through the transition.

Real-life Application: Apply these skills in managing real organizational changes, balancing support for your team with the necessity of the change.

Scenario 5: Crisis Management

Role-play handling a crisis situation. Display calm leadership, making quick and firm decisions, while showing empathy for the team's stress and uncertainty.

Real-life Application: In actual crisis situations, use these skills to lead effectively, ensuring your team feels supported and guided.

Scenario 6: Negotiating with Stakeholders

Simulate a negotiation with a difficult stakeholder or client. Practice standing firm on your organization's interests while understanding and addressing the stakeholder's needs.

Real-life Application: Use these negotiation skills in real stakeholder interactions, balancing firm advocacy for your organization with understanding of the stakeholder's perspective.

Through role-playing these scenarios and applying the learned skills in real-life situations, leaders can effectively develop and refine their ability to handle various challenges with a balance of firmness and empathy.

Incorporating mindfulness practices into daily routines enhances focus, reduces stress, and improves overall well-being. Here are some ways to integrate mindfulness into everyday life. Start the day with a mindfulness meditation. Spend a few minutes each morning focusing on your breath or doing a guided meditation to set a calm tone for the day. Practice mindful eating. Pay attention to the taste, texture, and aroma of your food. Eating slowly and without distractions can turn mealtimes into a mindfulness practice. Use transitional moments for deep breathing. In between tasks or meetings, take a few deep breaths to center yourself and clear your mind. Create mindful reminders. Set reminders on your phone or computer to pause and check-in with yourself throughout the day.

Engage in mindful movement. Activities like yoga or tai chi combine physical movement with mindfulness, but even a mindful walk, paying attention to each step and your surroundings, can be beneficial. Mindful listening in conversations. Focus fully on the person speaking, observing their words, tone, and body language without planning your response. Practice gratitude. Take time each day to think about things you are grateful for. This can shift your focus to positive aspects of your life and cultivate a mindful attitude. Perform routine tasks mindfully. Choose an everyday task like washing dishes or showering and do it with full attention to the sensations and actions involved. Mindful commuting. Use your commute to practice mindfulness. If you're driving, notice the feel of the steering wheel, the road sounds. If you're a passenger, observe the world passing by without judgment. End your day reflectively. Spend a few minutes before bed reflecting on the day, acknowledging your thoughts and feelings without criticism.

Incorporating these mindfulness practices into your daily routine can help you stay present, reduce stress, and improve your overall quality of life.

Managing stress and maintaining calm in leadership is vital for effective decision-making and overall well-being. Here are techniques to help leaders manage stress:

1. Practice regular relaxation techniques such as deep breathing, progressive muscle relaxation, or meditation. These methods help in reducing tension and promoting a sense of calm.

2. Establish a consistent exercise routine. Physical activity is effective in reducing stress hormones and releasing endorphins, improving mood and energy levels.

3. Ensure adequate sleep. Prioritize a healthy sleep schedule as it is crucial for stress management and cognitive function.

4. Develop time management skills. Organize and prioritize tasks to reduce the feeling of being overwhelmed. Learn to delegate where appropriate.

5. Cultivate a support network. Maintain open communication with peers, mentors, or a professional coach for support and guidance.

6. Implement mindfulness practices into daily routines, such as mindful walking or mindful eating, to stay present and reduce anxiety.

7. Learn to recognize stress triggers and develop proactive strategies for coping with them before they escalate.

8. Take regular breaks throughout the day, even short ones, to step away from work and recharge.

9. Practice positive self-talk and maintain a positive outlook. Reframing challenges and focusing on solutions rather than problems can reduce stress.

10. Engage in hobbies or activities outside of work that bring joy and relaxation, helping to maintain a work-life balance.

By regularly practicing these techniques, leaders can effectively manage stress, maintain calm, and enhance their ability to lead with clarity and composure.

Creating and nurturing a team culture that reflects Zen principles involves fostering an environment of mindfulness, balance, and harmony. This can be achieved by:

- Encouraging mindfulness practices within the team, such as starting meetings with a moment of silence or breathing exercises to promote presence and focus.

- Promoting a balanced approach to work, where productivity is valued but not at the expense of well-being. Encourage regular breaks and respect for work-life boundaries.

- Creating a peaceful and organized physical workspace, which can help in reducing stress and enhancing focus.

- Fostering open and honest communication. Encourage team members to express their thoughts and feelings in a respectful and constructive manner.

- Cultivating a sense of team unity and support, where collaboration is preferred over competition, and successes are celebrated together.

- Implementing regular team activities that focus on relaxation and well-being, such as group yoga sessions, mindfulness workshops, or team retreats.

- Encouraging reflective practices, like periodic reviews of team goals and processes, with a focus on continuous improvement and learning.

- Modeling Zen-like leadership by being calm, approachable, and thoughtful in decision-making, setting the tone for the team.

- Emphasizing the importance of empathy and understanding in team interactions, encouraging members to consider each other's perspectives and needs.

By integrating these practices into the team's routine, a culture that reflects Zen principles can be cultivated, leading to a more harmonious, productive, and positive work environment.

Encouraging open dialogue and mutual respect in a team involves creating an environment where all members feel valued and heard. This can be achieved by facilitating regular team meetings focused on open communication, where everyone is encouraged to share their ideas and perspectives. Leaders should actively listen to their team members, showing genuine interest in their contributions. Establishing ground rules for respectful interactions, such as not interrupting and acknowledging different viewpoints, is also essential.

Emphasizing the ongoing nature of becoming a Zen Master in leadership involves recognizing that this is a continuous journey of personal and professional growth. It requires consistent practice and commitment to the principles of mindfulness, balance, and self-awareness. Leaders should engage in regular self-reflection and seek feedback to understand their progress and areas for development. They should also be open to learning from various experiences and challenges, seeing them as opportunities for growth. Encouraging this mindset within the team can create a culture of continuous learning and improvement.

To conclude the chapter, we extend a strong encouragement for continuous learning and growth in the journey towards Zen Mastery in leadership. This path is not a destination but an ongoing process of personal and professional development. Leaders are urged to remain committed to their growth, embracing new experiences and challenges as opportunities to deepen their understanding and practice of Zen principles. Regular self-reflection, openness to feedback, and a willingness to adapt and change are key to this journey. By fostering a culture of continuous learning and encouraging team members to embark on their paths of growth, leaders can cultivate an environment where mindfulness, balance, and harmony thrive, leading to more effective, compassionate, and insightful leadership. This commitment to ongoing development not only enhances individual leadership skills but also contributes to the overall growth and success of the team and organization.

Part III: "The Gandhi of the Boardroom: Enlightened Leadership"

"Do or do not, there is no try." – Yoda

"The greatest teacher, failure is." – Yoda

"In my experience, there's no such thing as luck."
- Obi-Wan Kenobi -

Welcome to an exploration of enlightened leadership, a concept that redefines the traditional notions of authority in the business world.

We begin with Chapter 9, titled "Why Light is the New Black in Leadership." This chapter introduces us to the fundamental principles of Light Leadership. It's a revelation about how empathy, transparency, and a focus on collective well-being can elevate a leader's effectiveness far beyond the reach of conventional methods.

Moving on to Chapter 10, "Building Utopia: Creating Happy Workplaces," we delve into the art of transforming workplaces. This chapter is not just about productivity; it's about creating environments brimming with joy and creativity, outlining practical strategies for leaders to cultivate positive and thriving work cultures.

In Chapter 11, "Sunshine Stories: When Good Prevails," we share heartening stories from the real world. These are tales of leaders who have embraced Light Leadership and the significant impact their approach has had on both individuals and organizations.

Concluding this section, Chapter 12, "The Path to Enlightenment: How to Be a Light Leader," serves as a practical guide. It offers a step-by-step approach for those aspiring to embody the qualities of an enlightened leader.

Chapter 9: "Why Light is the New Black in Leadership"

In this chapter, we introduce the concept of Light Leadership, a transformative approach that is rapidly gaining traction in the modern business world. Light Leadership is defined by its emphasis on positivity, transparency, inspiration, and a forward-thinking mindset. This approach contrasts with traditional leadership models that often rely on authority, hierarchy, and control. Light Leadership represents a paradigm shift, focusing on empowering and uplifting team members, fostering innovation, and cultivating a culture of openness and collaboration.

The origin of Light Leadership can be traced to the evolving needs of today's workforce and the increasing importance of emotional intelligence, employee well-being, and ethical practices in the business environment. This leadership style is a response to the growing demand for leaders who are not only goal-oriented but also empathetic, authentic, and socially responsible.

Throughout this chapter, we will contrast Light Leadership with more conventional leadership models, highlighting how this approach is better suited to the dynamic and interconnected nature of contemporary business. We will explore the key characteristics of Light Leaders, their impact on organizational culture, and the benefits they bring to both employees and the broader business landscape.

The objectives of this chapter are to provide a comprehensive understanding of Light Leadership, demonstrate its effectiveness in various organizational contexts, and offer practical guidance for embracing and implementing this style in your own leadership practice. By the end of the chapter, readers will be equipped with the knowledge and tools to transform their leadership approach, harnessing the power of positivity, transparency, and inspiration to drive success and innovation.

Tracing the historical evolution of leadership styles is like journeying through the annals of human civilization, witnessing how leadership morphed and adapted to the social, economic, and technological shifts of each era.

In the early chapters of organized societies, the story of leadership was often one of authoritarian rule. Picture kings, tribal chiefs, and monarchs, whose words were law, and whose power was unchallenged. This era's leadership was built on a rigid hierarchy, with decisions cascading from the lofty heights of power to the masses below. Then came the seismic changes of the Industrial Revolution, a period that redefined not just industries but the very essence of leadership. The focus turned sharply towards efficiency, standardization, and productivity. The leaders of this age were more managers than monarchs, orchestrating a complex symphony of labor where control and organization were paramount. The theories of this era, like Taylor's Scientific Management, mirrored this mechanistic view of labor and leadership.

As the 20th century dawned, a new act began in the drama of leadership – the Human Relations Movement. Pioneers like Elton Mayo took center stage, spotlighting the human elements of the workforce – their needs, well-being, morale, and relationships. This was a pivotal turn, acknowledging that the cogs in the industrial machine had hearts and minds influencing their productivity. The post-World War II era heralded a shift towards more democratic shores. Leadership became participative, valuing team input, collaboration, and shared decision-making. This was a stark departure from the autocratic styles that had dominated the past, a fresh breeze of democracy blowing through the corridors of power.

As the late 20th century unfurled, new leadership theories like transformational and transactional leadership emerged. The former was a dance of inspiration and motivation, leading employees to transcend their own self-interests for the greater good, while the latter hinged on the pragmatic exchange between leader and follower, focusing on performance and efficiency. The 1990s brought with it a wave that emphasized the emotional quotient in leadership. Pioneered by thinkers like Daniel Goleman, this era put the spotlight on self-awareness, empathy, and interpersonal skills, adding a new dimension to the leader's toolkit.

Now, in the 21st century, the narrative of leadership is being rewritten yet again. It's more adaptive, inclusive, and focused on nurturing a positive organizational culture. Concepts like servant leadership, which emphasizes the growth and welfare of teams, and authentic leadership, focusing on ethics and transparency, are gaining prominence. In the digital age, leadership has entered a global, virtual arena. Today's leaders navigate a diverse and interconnected world, harnessing technology for communication and collaboration, leading teams that are as likely to be found across the globe as in the office next door.

The historical tapestry of leadership styles beautifully illustrates our growing understanding of the complex tapestry of human motivation and the evolving needs of organizations. From rigid, top-down models to flexible, people-centric approaches, the journey of leadership mirrors the journey of humanity itself – constantly evolving, learning, and adapting to the changing tides of time.

The evolution from authoritative to inclusive leadership has been significantly influenced by socio-economic changes across several dimensions. The transition from an industrial economy to an information and service-based economy has reshaped the nature of work, necessitating leadership styles that encourage creativity, problem-solving, and collaboration. Globalization has brought diverse cultures into the workplace, requiring leaders to manage and leverage the strengths of a global workforce.

Technological advancements have flattened organizational structures and democratized information flow, supporting more inclusive and participative leadership styles. The workforce now comprises multiple generations, each with its own set of expectations and work styles. Younger generations, such as Millennials and Gen Z, often seek meaningful work, work-life balance, and a collaborative environment, influencing a shift towards more inclusive leadership. There is also an increased public awareness of social justice, environmental sustainability, and ethical practices. Businesses are now expected to adopt responsible and sustainable practices, necessitating leaders who consider the broader impact of their decisions.

Economic shifts and labor market changes, highlighted by events like the 2008 financial crisis and the COVID-19 pandemic, have emphasized the need for adaptable and empathetic leadership to navigate through periods of uncertainty and change. Furthermore, with greater access to education and information, the workforce is more informed and empowered than ever before, leading to expectations of more participative decision-making processes. The rise of social media has increased organizational transparency, holding leaders accountable for their actions and policies. This public scrutiny supports leadership that is more inclusive, ethical, and socially responsible. These socio-economic factors collectively have steered the leadership evolution, favoring a style that values employee input, fosters collaboration, and adapts to the dynamic global business landscape.

The core principles of Light Leadership encompass a range of practices that prioritize positive, forward-thinking, and people-centered approaches: Empathy stands at the forefront, emphasizing the importance of understanding and connecting with team members. A Light Leader strives to see situations from their team members' perspectives, valuing their feelings and experiences. This approach not only enhances team morale but also fosters a deeper sense of loyalty and collaboration.

Transparency is another key tenet, where fostering trust through openness and honesty is critical. Light Leaders share information freely, keep their team informed about organizational changes, and are candid about challenges. This transparency cultivates an environment of trust and respect, where team members feel valued and included in the organization's journey.

Collective well-being is also a central aspect of Light Leadership. This principle is about prioritizing the happiness and success of the team as a whole. It involves creating a supportive work environment, encouraging work-life balance, recognizing and celebrating achievements, and attending to the team's professional and personal growth. By focusing on the collective well-being, Light Leaders ensure that the team not only excels in their tasks but also thrives in their work environment.

Empirical evidence supporting Light Leadership is found in various case studies across industries, demonstrating its effectiveness. One notable case study involves a tech startup that adopted Light Leadership principles. The leadership focused on transparency, empathy, and collective well-being. This approach led to a significant increase in employee engagement and innovation, as well as a reduction in turnover rates. The startup quickly outpaced its competitors in both employee satisfaction and market growth. In the healthcare sector, a hospital implementing Light Leadership witnessed remarkable improvements in patient care and staff morale. The administration's emphasis on open communication, empathetic management, and prioritizing staff well-being resulted in higher patient satisfaction scores and a more cohesive, motivated staff team.

A multinational corporation's shift to Light Leadership was documented in a case study that highlighted increased global team collaboration and productivity. The leaders' commitment to transparency and collective well-being, along with a strong emphasis on understanding cultural differences, led to more effective global operations and improved inter-departmental relationships. In education, a school district embracing Light Leadership principles observed notable improvements in both teacher performance and student outcomes. The district's focus on empathetic leadership, transparent communication, and the collective well-being of staff and students fostered a more supportive and productive educational environment.

These case studies underscore the effectiveness of Light Leadership in various contexts, showing how a leadership style focused on empathy, transparency, and collective well-being can lead to enhanced performance, improved employee satisfaction, and overall organizational success. Research findings consistently show a strong correlation between employee satisfaction and productivity, highlighting the impact of leadership styles and workplace environment on these outcomes:

1. Impact of Leadership Style: Studies have found that leadership styles emphasizing empathy, support, and empowerment tend to result in higher employee satisfaction. Leaders who practice open communication, recognize employee contributions, and encourage professional growth contribute to a more positive workplace atmosphere, enhancing satisfaction and motivation.

2. Workplace Environment and Employee Engagement: Research indicates that a positive workplace environment, where employees feel valued and part of a team, significantly boosts engagement. Engaged employees typically show higher levels of productivity, as they are more committed to the organization's goals and motivated to contribute their best.

3. Role of Autonomy and Empowerment: Empirical studies suggest that when employees are given autonomy and are empowered to make decisions, their job satisfaction and productivity increase. This sense of ownership and responsibility can lead to more innovative solutions and a more proactive approach to work.

4. Effects of Work-Life Balance: Research shows that work-life balance is a crucial factor in employee satisfaction. Organizations that support work-life balance through flexible working arrangements or other means tend to have more satisfied and productive employees.

5. Relationship Between Job Satisfaction and Productivity: A significant body of research supports the idea that job satisfaction positively impacts productivity. Satisfied

employees are often more efficient, have lower absenteeism rates, and are less likely to leave the organization, leading to reduced turnover costs and better continuity in teams.

6. Importance of Recognition and Reward Systems: Studies highlight the importance of effective recognition and reward systems in enhancing employee satisfaction. Recognition for achievements, whether through formal rewards or informal acknowledgement, can significantly boost morale and, consequently, productivity.

7. Mental Health and Well-being: Increasingly, research is focusing on the impact of mental health and overall well-being on employee productivity. Workplaces that prioritize mental health, offer support systems, and foster a positive work environment report higher levels of employee satisfaction and productivity.

These findings underscore the importance of leadership approaches and workplace practices that focus on creating a supportive, empowering, and positive environment, as these factors are key drivers of employee satisfaction and productivity. Real-world examples of successful Light Leaders demonstrate how this leadership style has been effectively implemented across various sectors:

In the technology industry, a CEO renowned for their empathetic and transparent leadership style has successfully guided their company through rapid growth and innovation. Their focus on open communication, employee well-being, and fostering a culture of inclusivity and collaboration has led to high employee satisfaction and sustained business success. In the non-profit sector, a leader has made significant strides in their organization's impact by prioritizing transparent communication and collective well-being. Their empathetic approach to both staff and the communities they serve has resulted in increased funding, successful campaigns, and a strong, motivated team.

A principal of a progressive school has become a model of Light Leadership in education. By fostering an environment of empathy, open dialogue, and prioritizing the well-being of both students and teachers, they have seen remarkable improvements in student engagement, academic performance, and teacher retention. In healthcare, a hospital administrator known for their Light Leadership approach has transformed the hospital's culture. Their emphasis on transparent communication, understanding the needs of both patients and staff, and creating a supportive work environment has led to improved patient care, staff satisfaction, and operational efficiency. A corporate leader in the finance sector has been recognized for their Light Leadership style. By focusing on transparency in communication, empathetic engagement with employees, and a commitment to the collective well-being of the team, they have cultivated a positive workplace culture that has driven both employee satisfaction and financial performance.

These examples across diverse sectors highlight the effectiveness of Light Leadership in creating positive work environments, driving organizational success, and fostering a culture where employees feel valued, motivated, and committed to their organization's vision and goals.

Not only the efficiency, but also the outcomes and impacts of Light Leadership, as demonstrated by this real-world example, reveal a significant positive effect on both organizational performance and employee well-being.

In the technology sector, a story unfolds that exemplifies the transformative power of empathetic and transparent leadership. At the heart of this narrative is a tech company that embraced a leadership approach marked by empathy and openness, which catalyzed a remarkable change within the organization and its workforce. This company, once navigating the typical challenges of the fast-paced tech world, decided to pivot its leadership style. The leaders chose to focus on understanding and addressing the needs and aspirations of their employees. They fostered a culture where open communication was not just encouraged but celebrated, and where employee feedback shaped policies and practices.

The impact of this empathetic and transparent leadership was profound. Employees, feeling heard and valued, became more engaged in their work. This heightened engagement sparked a surge in innovation and productivity, as team members felt empowered to bring forward new ideas and take creative risks. The company's open and inclusive culture began to attract top talent. Skilled professionals, drawn by the promise of a workplace that valued their input and well-being, flocked to join the company. This influx of talent further fueled innovation and growth, giving the company a competitive edge in the technology sector.

The ripple effect of this leadership transformation extended beyond employee engagement and talent attraction. The company's reputation grew, not just as a leader in technological innovation but also as a pioneer in progressive workplace culture. Their approach demonstrated a critical lesson: that empathetic and transparent leadership is not a mere idealistic pursuit, but a pragmatic strategy for driving sustainable growth and success in the technology industry. This narrative in the tech sector stands as a shining example of how leadership, when grounded in empathy and transparency, can create a thriving, innovative, and productive work environment, showcasing the indelible link between the nature of leadership and the success of an organization.

These outcomes collectively highlight the effectiveness of Light Leadership in fostering environments that encourage innovation, collaboration, and a strong sense of community. By prioritizing empathy, transparency, and collective well-being, Light Leaders create workplaces where employees are motivated, engaged, and aligned with the organization's goals, leading to improved performance and success.

Common misconceptions about Light Leadership often stem from a lack of understanding of its principles and effectiveness. One misconception is that Light Leadership is too soft or lenient, potentially leading to a lack of discipline or control within the organization. Critics might assume that focusing on empathy and well-being could compromise authority or the ability to make tough decisions. Another misconception is that Light Leadership may not be suitable for all industries or corporate cultures, particularly in more traditional or highly competitive sectors. There's a belief that this leadership style is more applicable to creative or progressive industries.

Some view Light Leadership as a trendy or faddish approach that lacks substance and long-term viability. They might see it as a passing phase rather than a sustainable leadership strategy. There's also a misunderstanding that Light Leadership avoids conflict or challenging conversations, mistaking its empathetic and inclusive approach for conflict avoidance.

Another common misconception is that Light Leadership is less about results and more about feelings, suggesting that it might not be as effective in driving organizational performance and achieving business goals. These misconceptions overlook the holistic nature of Light Leadership, which, while centered on empathy and transparency, also emphasizes accountability, performance, and effective decision-making. It's a balanced approach that fosters a positive work environment without compromising on discipline, results, or adaptability to different industries.

The journey of implementing Light Leadership within organizations, a narrative that contrasts sharply with traditional leadership models, is strewn with a unique set of challenges. This story begins in the hallways of companies where hierarchical and authoritative leadership styles have long been the norm. Here, the introduction of a more empathetic and inclusive approach is often met with resistance. Skepticism echoes through the ranks, from employees to managers, as they face the unfamiliar territory of new practices.

Picture a scene where a leader tries to infuse empathy into daily interactions, only to be confronted with the delicate task of balancing this empathy with the necessity of maintaining high performance and accountability. In this scenario, there's an underlying tension, a risk that empathy might be misconstrued as leniency, potentially leading to a relaxed grip on accountability and performance standards. The plot thickens in certain corporate cultures, particularly those that thrive on competition and results. In these settings, the principles of Light Leadership can seem like a foreign language, clashing with long-established norms and values. The challenge here is not just about introducing a new style of leadership but about reshaping the very fabric of the organizational culture.

An integral aspect involves the training and development needed to equip leaders and managers with the skills central to Light Leadership. This chapter highlights the investment of time and resources required to impart knowledge and skills in emotional intelligence, active listening, and transparent communication. Another significant challenge is the measurement of Light Leadership's impact. Unlike traditional models where success is often quantifiable, the benefits of Light Leadership are more qualitative, such as enhanced employee satisfaction or a more positive workplace culture. This subtlety in measuring impact adds complexity to the story.

Ensuring the consistent application of Light Leadership principles, especially in large or geographically dispersed organizations, presents its own set of trials. This is about maintaining uniformity and commitment to these principles across different teams and locations, ensuring that the ethos of Light Leadership is not lost in translation.

How then does the leader overcome these challenges of implementing Light Leadership? There are several aspects each of which must be carefully attended to including:

1. Educate and Communicate: Clearly communicate the benefits and principles of Light Leadership to the organization. Education and open dialogue can help in alleviating

skepticism and building a shared understanding of the value of this leadership approach.

2. Leadership Training: Invest in training programs that focus on developing skills essential for Light Leadership, such as emotional intelligence, empathetic communication, and conflict resolution. This can help leaders to balance empathy with accountability effectively.

3. Gradual Implementation: Introduce Light Leadership practices gradually, especially in organizations with a strong traditional leadership culture. This allows for a smoother transition and gives employees time to adapt to the new style.

4. Lead by Example: Senior leaders and managers should model Light Leadership behaviors. Demonstrating these practices in action can encourage acceptance and adoption throughout the organization.

5. Measure and Showcase Success: Develop metrics to measure the impact of Light Leadership, such as employee engagement surveys or productivity indicators. Sharing success stories and positive outcomes can further support the transition.

6. Foster a Supportive Culture: Create an organizational culture that supports the principles of Light Leadership. This includes recognizing and rewarding behaviors that align with empathy, transparency, and collective well-being.

7. Tailor Approaches: Recognize that one size does not fit all. Adapt the principles of Light Leadership to fit the unique context and culture of different parts of the organization.

By employing these strategies, organizations can effectively navigate the challenges of implementing Light Leadership and harness its potential to create a positive, collaborative, and high-performing work environment.

The influence of Light Leadership on organizational culture is profound and multifaceted. It reshapes the workplace environment, fostering a culture that is more collaborative, transparent, and people-focused. By prioritizing empathy, Light Leadership creates a more compassionate and understanding workplace. Employees feel valued and respected, which enhances job satisfaction and morale. This empathetic approach also improves team dynamics, encouraging a more supportive and cohesive work environment.

Transparency under Light Leadership builds trust within the organization. When leaders are open about decisions, challenges, and the company's direction, it fosters a culture of honesty and integrity. Employees feel more secure and involved, leading to greater commitment and loyalty. The emphasis on collective well-being contributes to a more positive and healthier workplace. This approach prioritizes not just business outcomes but also the personal and professional development of employees. It leads to a more balanced work-life culture, reducing burnout and improving overall job satisfaction.

Light Leadership also encourages innovation and creativity. By valuing diverse perspectives and fostering an inclusive environment, new ideas are encouraged and valued. This leads to a more dynamic and adaptable organization, capable of thriving in a rapidly changing business landscape. The influence of Light Leadership on organizational culture is transformative, creating a work environment that is not only productive and efficient but also nurturing and inclusive, leading to sustained organizational success and employee well-being.

We introduce case studies here that describe the organizational transformation under Light Leadership and demonstrate its profound impact.

A technology company facing high turnover and low morale shifted to Light Leadership, emphasizing empathy and transparency. This led to improved employee engagement, innovation, and a significant reduction in turnover. The company subsequently reported higher productivity and better market adaptability. In the retail sector, a major chain implemented Light Leadership principles, focusing on employee well-being and open communication. The result was a remarkable improvement in customer service ratings, employee satisfaction, and a boost in sales, as employees felt more valued and motivated.

A manufacturing firm struggling with efficiency and worker dissatisfaction adopted Light Leadership, prioritizing collective well-being and transparent decision-making. This shift resulted in enhanced teamwork, increased productivity, and a more positive workplace culture, ultimately improving both employee satisfaction and operational efficiency. A healthcare organization transformed its culture under Light Leadership by focusing on empathetic patient care and transparent management. This led to higher patient satisfaction scores, improved staff morale, and better healthcare outcomes, showcasing the impact of empathetic and transparent leadership in a high-stress environment.

These case studies illustrate how adopting Light Leadership can lead to positive outcomes across different industries, including higher employee satisfaction, improved efficiency, better customer service, and overall organizational success.

The adoption of Light Leadership within companies and its impact on employees unfolds as a story of significant and multifaceted benefits that reverberate through every level of an organization.

Light Leadership, with its positive and supportive ethos, cultivates a work environment where employees are more invested, motivated, and connected to their work, a key ingredient for long-term success and growth. The inclusive and open communication style championed by Light Leadership creates fertile ground for creative thinking and problem-solving, fostering a culture where innovative ideas can flourish. Companies practicing Light Leadership witness a decline in turnover, saving significant costs that otherwise would have been spent on recruitment and training. This stability is invaluable in building a strong, experienced workforce.

Then comes the enhancement of the company's reputation. Organizations known for their positive leadership approach and nurturing work culture become magnets for top talent. They are also often viewed favorably by consumers, enhancing their standing in the industry. Light Leadership, with its emphasis on adaptability and resilience, prepares organizations to navigate and thrive in an ever-evolving business landscape.

For employees, this kind of leadership translates into a myriad of benefits. It starts with heightened job satisfaction. In such nurturing and inclusive environments, employees report greater contentment and fulfillment in their roles. Light Leadership is synonymous with growth and learning, offering employees opportunities to enhance their skills and advance their careers. The focus on collective well-being and work-life balance under Light Leadership reduces stress and enhances overall mental and physical health. Enhanced workplace relationships also play a crucial role. This leadership style fosters collaboration and empathy, leading to stronger and more positive relationships among coworkers, enhancing team dynamics and productivity.

Working in an environment that values transparency and collective success fosters a deeper connection to their work and the company. Light Leadership reveals a cycle of positivity and success, highlighting its substantial impact on organizational health and employee well-being, and underscoring its importance as a transformative approach in modern business practices.

Developing empathy, transparency, and a focus on collective well-being in a business context involves adopting certain practices and exercises that enhance these qualities in leadership and team dynamics.

To cultivate empathy, it's essential to practice active listening. This means engaging fully in conversations and giving undivided attention to what others are saying, rather than thinking about a response while others are speaking. Implementing role reversal exercises can also be beneficial, as it encourages putting oneself in others' shoes, fostering a deeper understanding of their perspectives and feelings. Additionally, reflective journaling about daily interactions can be a powerful tool for improving empathetic responses, allowing for self-assessment and growth in how empathy is demonstrated in various situations.

For fostering transparency, establishing open communication channels is key. This can be achieved by setting up regular team meetings or feedback sessions that encourage open dialogue. Sharing the decision-making process with your team is also crucial; this involves explaining the rationale behind decisions, including the challenges faced and the trade-offs considered. Furthermore, encouraging honest feedback from team members and creating a safe space for them to express their thoughts and concerns without fear of repercussions can significantly enhance transparency within the team.

Promoting collective well-being involves regular check-ins with team members, where discussions go beyond work-related topics to include their well-being and professional aspirations. Organizing team-building activities can strengthen the sense of community and support among team members. Additionally, offering well-being workshops or training sessions that focus on stress management, work-life balance, and mental health can have a profound impact on the overall well-being of the team.

By integrating these practices into the leadership approach, organizations can effectively build a leadership style and a team culture that prioritizes empathy, transparency, and collective well-being. This approach not only enhances the work environment but also contributes to the overall productivity and satisfaction of the team.

The future evolution of leadership styles is anticipated to continue its trajectory towards more adaptive, empathetic, and collaborative models. Key trends likely to shape the landscape of leadership are varied and discussed here. For example, a heightened focus on emotional intelligence is expected, where leadership styles will prioritize empathy, self-awareness, and interpersonal skills more than ever before. This shift acknowledges the critical role of emotional intelligence in effective leadership. Flexibility and adaptability will become even more crucial as the pace of change in business and technology quickens. Leaders will need to be agile, ready to pivot in response to new challenges and opportunities that arise.

Inclusivity and diversity will increasingly be at the forefront of leadership. A growing recognition of the value of diverse perspectives and experiences will lead to more inclusive decision-making and problem-solving approaches. The rise of remote and hybrid leadership models will adapt to the growing trend of remote and hybrid work environments. Leadership styles will evolve to manage and engage teams that are not physically co-located, addressing the unique challenges of distributed work.

Sustainability and social responsibility will become more integral to leadership roles. As societal expectations evolve, leaders will focus more on ethical practices, environmental sustainability, and contributing positively to society. Data-driven decision-making will play a larger role in leadership. Leaders will increasingly rely on data and analytics to inform their decisions, blending these insights with their intuition and experience.

Lifelong learning will be emphasized due to the rapid evolution of knowledge and skills required for effective leadership. Continuous learning and development will be necessary to stay relevant and effective. The blending of professional and personal leadership will continue, with a diminishing line between the two. Leaders will be expected to bring their whole selves to their roles, emphasizing authenticity and vulnerability.

These trends suggest a future where leadership is more dynamic and human-centered, aligning closely with the changing needs of the workforce and broader society. This evolution points to a leadership paradigm that is not only more effective in achieving organizational goals but also more responsive to the well-being and development of individuals and communities.

The increasing relevance of Light Leadership in today's workplace is driven by a convergence of societal, technological, and economic changes. As Millennials and Gen Z become more predominant in the workforce, their preferences for a collaborative, inclusive, and empathetic work culture are reshaping leadership styles. These generations place a high value on workplaces that embody these qualities, steering away from traditional, hierarchical models.

In the context of globalization, businesses are operating across diverse cultural landscapes. This global footprint necessitates a leadership style that is adept at navigating a variety of cultural norms and expectations. Light Leadership, with its focus on inclusivity and empathy, is particularly effective in such a multicultural environment. The digital revolution and the rise of remote working paradigms call for a leadership style that adapts well to virtual environments. Light Leadership, emphasizing clear and compassionate communication, is well-suited for managing remote teams and ensuring connectedness despite physical distances.

There's an escalating emphasis on employee well-being, including mental health, within the workplace. Light Leadership aligns with this trend by prioritizing the mental and emotional health of employees, contributing to a more engaged and productive workforce. As ethical and sustainable business practices gain importance among consumers and employees, Light Leadership, which champions transparency and social responsibility, aligns perfectly with these emerging values.

The fast-paced nature of the current business landscape demands agility and innovation. Light Leadership creates an environment that encourages creativity and flexibility, essential for staying competitive and responsive to market changes. The growing recognition of the importance of emotional intelligence in leadership underscores the value of Light Leadership. This approach not only values but actively cultivates key emotional intelligence skills such as empathy, self-awareness, and effective relationship management.

The evolution of the modern workplace towards more inclusive, empathetic, and agile environments positions Light Leadership as a highly relevant and effective leadership style. It resonates with contemporary workforce values, embraces technological advancements, and aligns with the global shift towards ethical and innovative business practices.

The role of leadership in shaping a better future is pivotal and multifaceted. Effective leadership not only drives organizational success but also has a profound impact on societal and global progress. Leaders set the tone for their organizations, creating cultures that can either uplift or hinder human potential. By fostering environments of empathy, inclusivity, and innovation, leaders can unlock the collective talents and energies of their teams.

In today's interconnected world, the impact of leadership extends beyond organizational boundaries. Ethical and socially responsible leadership practices contribute to the greater good, addressing pressing global challenges like sustainability, equality, and social justice. Leaders who embrace adaptability and lifelong learning are better equipped to navigate the complexities of our rapidly changing world. They can lead their organizations through transformation and disruption, ensuring resilience and relevance.

The cultivation of emotional intelligence and ethical decision-making in leadership has far-reaching implications. These qualities are essential for addressing the nuanced challenges of our time and for making decisions that consider the long-term welfare of communities and the planet.

The chapter on Light Leadership encompassed several key points. Light Leadership was defined as a leadership style emphasizing positivity, transparency, inspiration, and forward-thinking, contrasting with more traditional, hierarchical models. The evolution of leadership styles was explored, highlighting the shift from authoritative to more inclusive and empathetic approaches, influenced by socio-economic changes.

Core principles of Light Leadership include empathy, transparency, and a focus on collective well-being, each contributing to a positive and productive organizational culture. Case studies and research findings provided evidence of the effectiveness of Light Leadership in enhancing employee satisfaction, innovation, and overall organizational performance. Misconceptions about Light Leadership, such as it being too lenient or not results-focused, were addressed and debunked. Challenges in implementing Light Leadership were discussed, along with strategies to overcome these, such as education, gradual implementation, and leading by example. The profound impact of Light Leadership on organizational culture was highlighted, showing its role in fostering collaborative, transparent, and inclusive environments.

Real-world examples demonstrated organizational transformations under Light Leadership, showcasing improvements in employee engagement, innovation, and productivity. The long-term benefits for both companies and employees were discussed, including enhanced engagement, innovation, job satisfaction, and organizational success. Practical tips and exercises for developing key Light Leadership skills like empathy, transparency, and a focus on collective well-being were provided. Predictions on how leadership styles will continue to evolve toward more adaptive, empathetic, and collaborative approaches were explored. The chapter concluded with suggestions for workshops and training programs aimed at developing skills necessary for aspiring Light Leaders.

Embracing Light Leadership principles can lead to transformative outcomes for both leaders and their organizations. These principles foster an environment of positivity, empathy, and inclusivity, essential for navigating the complexities of the modern workplace. By adopting Light Leadership, you can drive innovation, enhance team cohesion, and create a workplace culture that values and nurtures the potential of each individual.

Light Leadership also aligns with the evolving expectations of a diverse and global workforce, emphasizing the importance of emotional intelligence, ethical practices, and social responsibility. These qualities are increasingly recognized as critical components of effective leadership.

Moreover, incorporating Light Leadership into your leadership style can significantly contribute to your personal growth and professional development. It encourages a mindset of continuous learning, adaptability, and self-reflection, which are invaluable in personal and career advancement.

In a rapidly changing business landscape, Light Leadership offers a sustainable path forward, balancing the pursuit of organizational goals with the well-being and development of team members. It's an approach that not only leads to better business outcomes but also contributes to creating a more compassionate and equitable world. Therefore, there is a strong encouragement to explore and integrate Light Leadership principles into your leadership practice. It's a commitment not just to personal and organizational success, but to being a part of shaping a positive and progressive future.

The transformative power of Light Leadership lies in its ability to reshape not just organizations but also the individuals within them. By emphasizing empathy, transparency, and collective well-being, Light Leadership creates a nurturing and positive environment that encourages growth, innovation, and collaboration. It moves beyond traditional metrics of success to build workplaces where individuals feel valued, heard, and inspired to contribute their best.

This leadership approach is particularly pertinent in today's fast-paced, ever-changing global landscape. It equips leaders and organizations with the flexibility and resilience needed to navigate challenges and seize opportunities. The emphasis on emotional intelligence and ethical practices under Light Leadership fosters a culture of trust and integrity, essential in sustaining long-term success.

Light Leadership has the potential to drive societal change. By prioritizing inclusivity, empathy, and well-being, it sets a standard for how businesses can positively impact their communities and the wider world. In essence, Light Leadership is more than a leadership style; it's a commitment to a vision of leadership that values both human and organizational flourishing.

In closing, the call to embrace Light Leadership is a call to embrace a future where leadership is synonymous with compassion, innovation, and a deep sense of responsibility towards the greater good. It's an invitation to be part of a leadership movement that has the power to transform our workplaces, communities, and society for the better.

Chapter 10: "Building Utopia: Creating Happy Workplaces"

A 'Happy Workplace' is defined not just as a place where employees are satisfied with their jobs, but where they find genuine joy and fulfillment in their work. It encompasses elements like positive company culture, supportive management, meaningful work, opportunities for growth, work-life balance, and recognition of efforts. Research has consistently shown that happy employees are more productive, creative, and committed. They are also less likely to experience burnout, have fewer sick days, and are more likely to stay with their employer long-term. Thus, cultivating a happy workplace is not just beneficial for employees, but it's also a strategic advantage for organizations.

The focus of this chapter is to provide a comprehensive understanding of how to create and sustain a happy workplace. It aims to dissect the key components that contribute to employee happiness, backed by research and real-world examples. The goals include offering actionable strategies for leaders and managers to foster a happier work environment and illustrating the tangible benefits that such an environment brings to both employees and the organization as a whole. By the end of this chapter, readers should have a clear blueprint for building their own version of a workplace utopia, where happiness is a fundamental pillar.

Research findings consistently demonstrate a strong correlation between employee happiness and work output, underlining the importance of fostering a positive work environment. Happy employees are more productive. Studies have shown that when workers are satisfied and engaged, their speed and efficiency in task completion improves, boosting overall productivity. A happy work environment fosters creativity. Employees who feel content and valued are more likely to think creatively, contribute innovative ideas, and find effective solutions to problems.

Happier employees are less likely to take unscheduled time off and are more loyal to their employers. This reduces the costs and disruptions associated with high turnover and absenteeism. Happiness positively impacts the quality of work. Happy employees tend to be more attentive to detail and take greater pride in their work, leading to higher quality outputs.

Research indicates that happiness enhances decision-making skills. Happy employees make more accurate and effective decisions, as positivity improves cognitive function and problem-solving abilities. Happiness in the workplace fosters a collaborative spirit. Employees who are content and feel a sense of belonging are more likely to work effectively in teams, contributing to a harmonious and productive work environment. A happy work environment contributes to the overall mental and physical well-being of employees. This can lead to fewer health-related costs for the company and a more energetic, present workforce.

These research findings underscore the importance of employee happiness as a key factor in enhancing work output and overall organizational success. Investing in creating and sustaining a happy workplace is not just beneficial for employees but is also a strategic business decision.

A positive work environment brings a multitude of psychological benefits that significantly enhance the mental and emotional well-being of employees, impacting not just their professional life but their overall quality of life. In such an environment, employees often report a higher level of job satisfaction. This stems from feeling valued, supported, and engaged in purposeful work. The acknowledgment of their efforts and the sense of being part of something meaningful enhances their work experience.

Stress and anxiety, common in today's fast-paced work life, are notably reduced in a positive workplace setting. The supportive and understanding nature of such environments contributes to a more relaxed and enjoyable experience at work, allowing employees to perform their duties in a less pressured atmosphere.

Motivation levels see a marked increase in positive work settings. When employees feel that their contributions are recognized and appreciated, they are more driven to excel and bring their best efforts to the table. This motivation goes beyond mere financial incentives, tapping into intrinsic values and personal fulfillment. The mental health of employees is significantly improved in positive work environments. Such settings are characterized by lower risks of burnout and depression, fostering happier and more fulfilled employees. This not only benefits the individual's well-being but also enhances their productivity and engagement at work.

A sense of belonging and community is another key benefit. Positive work cultures create an atmosphere where employees feel connected, appreciated, and part of a cohesive team. This sense of belonging is crucial for building strong team dynamics and ensuring employee loyalty. Employees' self-esteem and confidence are bolstered in environments where their work is valued. Recognition and appreciation of their efforts lead to a positive self-image and greater confidence in their abilities, which in turn enhances their performance and willingness to take on new challenges.

Recognizing the importance of work-life balance is a hallmark of positive workplaces. Such environments acknowledge the significance of employees' lives outside of work, contributing to their mental and emotional health and preventing burnout. Resilience is nurtured in supportive work environments. Employees in such settings are better equipped to handle professional challenges and setbacks, thanks to the supportive culture and the resources available to them.

The psychological benefits of a positive work environment ripple through every aspect of organizational life. They contribute to healthier, more satisfied, and more productive employees, thereby enhancing team dynamics, enriching organizational culture, and driving overall company performance.

In the corporate world, several real-life case studies from various industries vividly illustrate the significant impact that workplace happiness can have on productivity.

In the tech industry, a major company introduced flexible working arrangements and wellness programs. The result was a noticeable increase in employee happiness. Following these changes, the company observed a substantial rise in productivity, including improved software development timelines and a spike in innovation.

In the retail sector, a chain implemented several employee happiness initiatives. These included staff recognition programs and enhanced team communication. The outcome was impressive, with a notable increase in sales performance, improved customer service ratings, and a reduction in staff turnover.

A manufacturing company took significant steps to create a happier workplace. They improved safety standards, offered professional development opportunities, and enhanced employee autonomy. This focus on employee well-being led to a marked increase in production efficiency and a notable decrease in workplace accidents.

In healthcare, a provider invested in employee satisfaction by supporting management and emphasizing work-life balance. The results were striking, with higher patient care ratings, increased employee retention, and improved operational efficiency.

An educational institution focused on fostering faculty and staff happiness through collaborative decision-making and a supportive work environment. This approach resulted in increased student satisfaction, improved academic performance, and better staff retention rates.

These cases across different sectors underscore the correlation between workplace happiness and enhanced productivity. They highlight that prioritizing employee well-being and satisfaction is not just a moral imperative but a strategic one, leading to tangible benefits like improved efficiency, higher retention, and overall organizational success. These examples serve as compelling evidence for businesses to consider workplace happiness as a key factor in their operational and strategic planning.

The role of leadership in fostering a positive work environment is critical and multifaceted. Leaders are responsible for setting the cultural tone of the organization. Their attitudes and behaviors often set a precedent that can influence the entire workplace atmosphere. Effective leaders articulate a clear vision that includes positivity as a core value. They champion the importance of a positive work environment in achieving organizational goals.

Leaders must embody the positivity they wish to see in their teams. Demonstrating qualities like optimism, resilience, and approachability encourages similar behaviors among employees. They also play a key role in recognizing and appreciating the contributions of their team members. This recognition can significantly boost morale and foster a sense of value and belonging. Encouraging transparent and open communication helps build trust and respect, which are essential for a positive work environment. Leaders who invest in the development of their employees, both professionally and personally, contribute to a more engaged and satisfied workforce.

Effective leaders address workplace challenges and conflicts in a constructive manner, promoting solutions that respect and consider the well-being of all parties involved. They can create a positive environment by promoting collaboration and teamwork, emphasizing the importance of working together towards common goals. Leaders who prioritize work-life balance help prevent burnout and stress, contributing to a healthier, more positive workplace.

By playing these roles, leaders can significantly influence the creation and maintenance of a positive work environment, leading to improved employee well-being, increased productivity, and overall organizational success.

The importance of work-life balance, recognition, and employee empowerment in the workplace is paramount, each playing a crucial role in fostering a productive and positive work environment:

Maintaining a healthy balance between work and personal life is essential for employee well-being. It helps prevent burnout and stress, leading to more engaged and satisfied employees. When employees feel they have time for personal pursuits and family, their job satisfaction and loyalty to the organization increase. This balance also contributes to better mental and physical health, reducing absenteeism and improving overall productivity.

Recognizing and appreciating employees for their hard work and achievements is a powerful motivator. It boosts morale, enhances self-esteem, and encourages employees to continue performing at their best. Recognition doesn't just mean financial rewards; it can also be verbal acknowledgment, opportunities for professional growth, or public appreciation. When employees feel valued, they are more likely to be committed to their job and the organization, leading to a more positive workplace culture and reduced turnover.

Empowering employees by giving them autonomy, authority, and trust to make decisions enhances job satisfaction and a sense of ownership. Empowered employees are more likely to take initiative, be creative, and feel invested in their work, which can lead to innovative solutions and improvements in processes. This empowerment also fosters a culture of trust and respect, as employees feel their opinions and contributions are valued and respected.

Together, work-life balance, recognition, and employee empowerment contribute significantly to creating a happy, productive, and sustainable workplace. They are key factors in attracting and retaining top talent and are essential for the long-term success of any organization.

Developing a positive and inclusive culture involves a series of strategic steps that focus on fostering respect, diversity, and a sense of community within the workplace. Actively work to create a diverse workforce. Implement policies and practices that ensure inclusivity in hiring, promotion, and everyday work activities. Celebrate diverse perspectives and backgrounds as a key strength of the organization. Create channels for transparent communication where employees can share ideas, express concerns, and offer feedback without fear of retribution. Regular team meetings, suggestion boxes, and open-door policies can facilitate this.

Offer training programs that focus on diversity, sensitivity, and effective communication to educate employees about the importance of an inclusive culture and how to contribute to it. Acknowledge and celebrate the successes and milestones of teams and individual employees. Recognition can take many forms, from formal awards to informal acknowledgments in meetings.

Encourage collaboration and team-building activities that allow employees to work together and understand each other's strengths and viewpoints. Ensure that all company policies, including those related to hiring, promotions, and remuneration, are fair and transparent. This reinforces a sense of fairness and equity in the workplace.

Leadership should embody the values of inclusivity and positivity. The behavior of leaders sets a tone for the rest of the organization, so it's crucial that they demonstrate the values they wish to see in their teams. Offer support mechanisms like mentoring programs, employee resource groups, and wellness initiatives that help build a supportive and inclusive environment. Ensure that the workplace is not only physically safe but also emotionally and psychologically supportive, where employees feel secure and valued.

By implementing these strategies, organizations can cultivate a positive and inclusive culture that values diversity, promotes open communication, and fosters a sense of belonging and community among all employees.

Organizational values and ethics are more than just corporate rhetoric; they are the bedrock upon which companies build their culture, influence behavior, and steer decision-making, deeply impacting employee happiness and workplace satisfaction.

Imagine a workplace where employees' personal values echo in the corridors of their organization. This alignment of personal and organizational values doesn't just resonate with employees; it imbues them with a sense of belonging and purpose. Such a congruence between what employees cherish personally and what their company stands for can significantly enhance job satisfaction, boosting morale and motivation.

Trust and integrity are the cornerstones of such organizations. When a company upholds high ethical standards, it weaves a fabric of trust among its employees. Knowing that their company operates with integrity and fairness doesn't just contribute to a sense of security; it instills pride in being part of the organization.

The role of ethical leadership in this narrative is pivotal. Leaders who exemplify ethical behavior and decision-making set a powerful precedent. Their actions foster a respectful and trustworthy environment where employees feel genuinely valued and treated fairly.

Consider the importance of respecting employee rights in this context. Ethical standards often manifest as equitable treatment of employees – fair compensation, reasonable working hours, and a steadfast stand against discrimination and harassment. These practices create a workplace that respects and honors its workforce.

Moreover, the commitment to social responsibility by companies often kindles a sense of pride among employees. Engaging in practices that contribute to societal good enriches the meaningfulness of their work, enhancing overall job satisfaction.

Ethical practices lay the groundwork for positive workplace relationships. They encourage transparency, open communication, and effective conflict resolution strategies, ensuring that all parties are respected and heard.

Lastly, consider the emphasis on employee well-being in ethically minded organizations. They often prioritize policies that support a healthy work-life balance, mental health, and opportunities for professional growth and development.

Several companies are renowned for their strong, positive cultures, setting benchmarks in various industries:

- Google: Known for its innovative and employee-friendly work environment, Google offers various perks like wellness programs, creative workspaces, and professional development opportunities. The company emphasizes a culture of openness, creativity, and collaboration, making it consistently one of the best places to work.

- Zappos: Famous for its unique company culture, Zappos prioritizes customer service and employee happiness. The company fosters a fun and inclusive work environment with a strong emphasis on company values and team building.

- Salesforce: Salesforce has been lauded for its culture of trust, transparency, and giving back. The company focuses on employee well-being and philanthropy, encouraging employees to participate in community service and providing benefits like wellness reimbursements.

- Patagonia: An outdoor apparel company, Patagonia is recognized for its commitment to environmental sustainability and work-life balance. The company offers flexible working arrangements and encourages employees to pursue outdoor activities, aligning with its brand ethos.

- Netflix: Netflix's culture is centered around freedom and responsibility. The company offers flexible work arrangements and emphasizes a culture of innovation, where employees are encouraged to take initiative and think creatively.

- Southwest Airlines: Known for its exceptional customer service, Southwest Airlines fosters a culture of employee empowerment and fun. The company values a positive work atmosphere and often goes above and beyond to ensure employee satisfaction.

These companies exemplify strong, positive cultures where employee happiness, well-being, and development are integral parts of their business philosophy, contributing to their success and industry-leading positions.

Enhancing employee engagement and satisfaction is a multifaceted approach that hinges on creating a positive and supportive work environment, tailored to meet the diverse needs of the workforce. At the forefront of this approach is personalized recognition. It's about acknowledging and appreciating the unique contributions of each employee. This form of individualized acknowledgment ensures that employees feel their efforts are not just seen but valued, enhancing their connection to their work and the organization.

Career development opportunities form another critical pillar in this strategy. Offering training programs, workshops, and clear pathways for career progression signifies an investment in employees' professional growth. This not only contributes to their sense of purpose within the company but also bolsters their overall job satisfaction. Effective communication is the lifeblood of employee engagement. Maintaining open channels where feedback and suggestions are not just welcomed but actively sought ensures employees feel heard and valued. It's about creating a dialogue where ideas and concerns can be freely expressed and addressed.

Empowerment and autonomy play a crucial role in job satisfaction. By entrusting employees with decision-making authority in their areas of expertise, organizations foster a sense of ownership and responsibility, which can lead to greater job satisfaction and commitment.

The role of fostering strong team relationships cannot be overstated. Encouraging teamwork and collaboration contributes significantly to a supportive work environment, enhancing job satisfaction and strengthening interpersonal connections. Acknowledging the importance of work-life balance is vital. Implementing flexible work arrangements and policies that respect employees' personal time demonstrates a commitment to their overall well-being.

Well-being programs focused on both physical and mental health are increasingly becoming a staple in the modern workplace. These might include wellness challenges, mental health days, and access to fitness facilities, all contributing to employees' overall health and productivity. An inclusive and positive workplace culture is a cornerstone of employee engagement. Cultivating an environment that values diversity and inclusivity ensures that all employees feel a sense of belonging and respect. Engaging leadership is key. Leaders and managers should be approachable and supportive, effectively guiding their teams with a focus on both performance and personal well-being.

By weaving these various strands into the fabric of their organizational culture, companies can significantly boost employee engagement and satisfaction, leading to a workforce that is not only more productive and motivated but also deeply committed to the organization's success.

Mental health in the workplace is an increasingly recognized and vital aspect of overall employee well-being and organizational success. In today's fast-paced and often high-pressure work environments, addressing and supporting mental health has become a critical priority.

The importance of mental health at work stems from its significant impact on both individuals and the organization. Employees who are mentally healthy tend to be more productive, engaged, and capable of managing stress effectively. They are also more likely to contribute positively to team dynamics, foster a supportive work culture, and demonstrate resilience in the face of workplace challenges. Conversely, when mental health is not prioritized, it can lead to increased absenteeism, reduced productivity, and higher turnover rates. Poor mental health can affect an employee's ability to make decisions, interact with colleagues, and perform their job effectively. It also has a broader impact on workplace morale and can contribute to a negative work environment.

Recognizing the importance of mental health, many organizations are now implementing strategies to support their employees. This includes providing access to mental health resources, such as counseling services or employee assistance programs. Workplaces are also increasingly focusing on creating a culture that reduces stigma around mental health, encouraging open conversations and offering support without judgment.

Leadership plays a crucial role in setting the tone for how mental health is perceived and addressed in the workplace. Leaders who prioritize their own mental well being and openly discuss the importance of mental health can foster a more open and supportive culture.

Mental health is a key component of employee well-being and organizational health. By acknowledging its importance and taking steps to foster a supportive environment, workplaces can not only improve the well-being of their employees but also enhance their overall productivity and success.

In recent times, forward-thinking organizations have been weaving a tapestry of programs and initiatives aimed at nurturing the well-being of their employees. At the heart of these efforts is a recognition of the intricate connection between an individual's well-being and their productivity at work.

Picture a typical day in such a workplace: it might begin with a yoga class or a mindfulness session, part of a comprehensive wellness program that recognizes the symbiotic relationship between physical and mental health. Employees stretch and breathe, preparing themselves not just for the challenges of the day but for a sustained, healthy work life.

In the corners of this workplace, you'll find quiet, comforting spaces dedicated to mental health support. Here, employees have access to counseling services, offering a safe haven for those grappling with both personal and professional challenges. It's not uncommon to see colleagues taking a mental health day off, a practice supported and even encouraged by the organization.

Flexibility is woven into the fabric of the workday. Employees have the freedom to choose their hours, work remotely, or even compress their workweeks. This flexibility acknowledges the diverse needs and life situations of each individual, fostering a culture where work-life balance isn't just a buzzword, but a lived reality.

Professional growth is nurtured through a myriad of opportunities. Workshops, training sessions, and skill development programs are regular features, fueling both the personal and professional growth of the employees. This investment in development often translates into a workforce that is not only skilled but also deeply satisfied and engaged in their work. Health and fitness are championed too. Employees have access to health insurance, gym memberships, or wellness stipends, promoting a culture that places a high premium on physical health.

Team-building activities and social events dot the calendar, creating opportunities for employees to bond, laugh, and engage in meaningful community work together. These activities knit the workforce into a close-knit community, where members feel valued and connected. Amidst all this, a system of recognition and reward pulses vibrantly, ensuring that hard work and achievements are celebrated. This system isn't just about financial incentives; it's about acknowledging the human effort and passion that drives the company forward.

Leaders and managers in this ecosystem are more than just taskmasters; they are trained to be empathetic, to recognize signs of stress and burnout in their teams, and to respond with understanding and support. They are the gardeners in this flourishing workplace, nurturing and caring for the growth around them. In such a workplace, programs like mindfulness and stress reduction aren't just add-ons; they are integral to the organizational culture. Employees are equipped with techniques to manage stress, leading to a more harmonious balance between work and life pressures.

This narrative isn't a utopian dream but a growing reality in many modern organizations. These companies have recognized that the well-being of their employees is not just a corporate responsibility, but also a cornerstone for sustained success and growth. They are the pioneers in crafting a workplace that doesn't just demand output but cares for the input – the human spirit and well-being.

The influence of physical space on employee mood and productivity is profound, with innovative office designs playing a pivotal role in promoting workplace happiness. The environment in which employees work can significantly affect their mental well-being, engagement, and efficiency.

Innovative office designs now often prioritize open spaces, natural light, and elements of nature. These designs are not just about aesthetics; they are about creating an environment that stimulates creativity and reduces stress. For instance, incorporating biophilic design, which integrates natural elements like plants, water features, and natural light, has been shown to reduce stress and improve mood and cognitive function.

Collaborative spaces are another key feature of modern office design. These spaces are designed to facilitate teamwork and communication, featuring comfortable seating, communal tables, and interactive whiteboards. However, alongside these collaborative areas, there's also a growing recognition of the need for quiet, private spaces where employees can focus on individual tasks without distractions. Ergonomics plays a critical role in office design. Ergonomically designed furniture and workstations not only reduce the risk of strain and injury but also enhance comfort, which can boost productivity and job satisfaction.

Color psychology is also employed in office design. Certain colors can evoke different emotional responses; for example, blues and greens are often used to create a calming atmosphere, while yellows can stimulate creativity and energy. To create a conducive and enjoyable work environment, here are some tips:

1. Ensure Adequate Natural Light: Maximize natural light in the workspace, as it has been proven to boost mood and energy levels.
2. Incorporate Greenery: Add plants to the office space. Plants not only improve air quality but also have a calming effect on employees.

3. Create Different Work Areas: Design different areas for collaboration, relaxation, and focused work to accommodate various work styles and needs.

4. Prioritize Ergonomics: Invest in comfortable and adjustable furniture to support physical well-being.

5. Use Color Wisely: Choose office colors that align with the desired mood and energy of the space.

6. Personalize the Space: Allow employees to personalize their workspace, which can increase their emotional connection and comfort.

7. Promote Cleanliness and Organization: A clean and organized workspace can reduce stress and improve focus.

8. Consider Acoustics: Good acoustics are important, especially in open-plan offices, to reduce noise levels and distractions.

By thoughtfully designing physical spaces that cater to the needs and well-being of employees, organizations can create environments that not only enhance productivity but also contribute to a happier and more satisfied workforce.

Balancing the diverse needs and expectations of employees is a complex yet crucial task for any organization aiming to foster a positive and inclusive workplace. Understanding that each employee brings their own set of values, experiences, and preferences is key. Leaders and managers should strive to accommodate these varied needs without compromising the overall organizational goals.

One effective approach is to actively engage in open dialogue with employees to understand their unique perspectives and needs. This can be achieved through regular feedback sessions, surveys, or informal conversations. Such engagement demonstrates a genuine interest in the employees' well-being and can provide valuable insights into how to create a more accommodating work environment. Flexible working arrangements are another critical factor. By offering options like remote work, flexible hours, and part-time opportunities, organizations can cater to a wide range of work-life balance preferences and personal commitments.

Professional development opportunities should also be diverse and inclusive, catering to different career aspirations and learning styles. Providing a variety of training programs, mentorship opportunities, and paths for advancement can help meet the varied growth and development needs of employees. Health and wellness programs should be comprehensive and holistic, addressing physical, mental, and emotional health. This might include offering gym memberships, wellness workshops, mental health support, and health insurance options that cover a broad range of services.

Cultural inclusivity is also essential. Celebrating different cultures, encouraging multilingual communication, and respecting diverse traditions and holidays can enhance the sense of belonging and respect among a diverse workforce.

Leadership styles should be adaptable and empathetic, capable of recognizing and responding to the different motivational drivers and communication preferences of various employees. Policies and practices around rewards and recognition should be fair and equitable, ensuring that they reflect the diverse contributions and achievements of all employees. By addressing these diverse needs and expectations, organizations can create a more harmonious and productive workplace where every employee feels valued and supported.

In the high-stress corridors of modern workplaces, where the ticking clock often races against mounting expectations, addressing burnout and stress has become a mission critical for organizations. The bustling pace, while a hallmark of efficiency and ambition, often casts a shadow – the looming threat of burnout. Recognizing and tackling this has become an art and a strategic imperative in high-pressure environments.

Imagine walking through the halls of such an organization, where leaders and managers are not just taskmasters, but guardians of their teams' well-being. Here, addressing burnout isn't an afterthought; it's woven into the fabric of the company's culture.

It begins with a keen awareness – managers trained to spot the early signs of stress and burnout. These are the workplaces where a prolonged gaze at the computer screen or a missed lunch break doesn't go unnoticed. The leadership understands that early intervention is key, and they act not just with directives, but with empathy and support.

Regular check-ins become more than just status updates. They are genuine inquiries into an employee's well-being, where conversations about workload, challenges, and personal hurdles are as commonplace as discussions about project deadlines. These are safe spaces where admitting stress isn't a sign of weakness, but a step towards collective strength.

In these high-pressure environments, the mantra is clear – take breaks before the breaks take you. Break rooms and relaxation spaces are sanctuaries of tranquility amidst the bustle. Here, employees find a moment of respite, a brief escape to recharge. Some organizations go further, offering meditation sessions or yoga classes, recognizing that mental health is as crucial as physical health.

Flexible work policies play a pivotal role too. The option to work from home or adjust hours isn't seen as a perk but as a necessary tool for balance. This flexibility acknowledges that productivity thrives not under rigid constraints, but in environments where personal and professional lives can coexist harmoniously.

Several real-life case studies highlight organizations that have successfully transformed their workplaces into hubs of happiness, significantly impacting employee satisfaction and productivity.

A multinational tech company, once plagued by high stress and burnout rates, implemented a comprehensive well-being program. They introduced flexible working hours, regular wellness workshops, and an open-door policy for mental health discussions. As a result, employee satisfaction scores soared, and productivity increased, setting a new benchmark in the tech industry for employee care.

A leading marketing firm, recognizing the toll of high-pressure campaigns on its staff, decided to overhaul its work culture. It started with mandatory breaks, mindfulness training, and retreats focused on team bonding and relaxation. The firm saw a remarkable decrease in turnover rates and a surge in creative output, garnering industry-wide attention for its innovative approach to employee well-being.

A healthcare provider, amid the intense demands of the sector, took a bold step to address staff burnout. They introduced shorter shifts, longer breaks, and a support system for emotional and mental health care. The changes led to improved patient care, as the staff were more focused and empathetic, showcasing the direct impact of employee happiness on service quality.

An international law firm, traditionally known for its grueling hours, initiated a "happiness project." This included unassigned work hours, where employees could pursue personal projects or professional development, and a mentorship program focusing on work-life balance. The firm not only retained its top talent but also attracted new recruits, eager to be part of a progressive work culture.

These case studies exemplify how varied organizations, by prioritizing employee happiness and well-being, can transform their work environments. These transformations lead to increased productivity, creativity, and overall job satisfaction, proving that a happy workplace is not just a utopian ideal, but a practical, achievable goal.

The journey of transforming workplaces into havens of happiness and productivity has imparted profound lessons and insights, echoing across the corridors of various industries. In this narrative of change and evolution, several themes have emerged, painting a picture of what it truly means to cultivate a workplace that thrives on the happiness of its employees.

At the forefront of this transformation is the undeniable realization that employee well-being must be a paramount priority. Companies that have embraced this ethos have not just enriched the lives of their employees but have also reaped the rewards in productivity and loyalty. It's a testament to the fact that caring for the workforce is not just a moral obligation but a smart business strategy.

The narrative also speaks volumes about the power of flexibility and work-life balance. Companies that have introduced flexible working arrangements have written success stories underlined by higher job satisfaction and reduced burnout rates. This flexibility has proven to be a cornerstone in building trust and understanding, fostering an environment where employees feel valued beyond their output.

Recognition emerges as a pivotal chapter in this story. Regular acknowledgment, whether through formal programs or simple gestures of appreciation, has shown to be a catalyst for employee motivation and morale. It's a reminder that every effort counts and deserves to be celebrated.

An inclusive and supportive culture stands as a strong pillar in these transformed workplaces. In these spaces, every individual, irrespective of their background or role, feels a sense of belonging and support. It's a culture where diversity is not just accepted but celebrated, creating a rich tapestry of ideas and perspectives.

Professional development and growth opportunities have also been key plot points in this narrative. Organizations that have invested in their employees' growth have witnessed not just the ascent of their workforce but also the elevation of their own standards and capabilities.

Leadership, in this story, plays the role of a guiding star. Leaders who demonstrate empathy, transparency, and support have been instrumental in steering their organizations towards a culture of positivity and respect. They set the stage for others to follow, embodying the values they wish to see in their teams.

Listening to employee feedback has been a recurring theme in these success stories. It highlights the importance of giving a voice to the workforce, ensuring that their opinions and suggestions shape the policies and practices of the company.

Finally, the narrative underscores the importance of sustainability in these efforts. The journey to a happy workplace is not a sprint but a marathon, requiring ongoing commitment and effort. It's a continuous process of nurturing and investing in the well-being of the workforce, understanding that this is the bedrock of long-term success and fulfillment.

Through these stories and lessons, a clear message resonates: the path to a happy and productive workplace is paved with empathy, flexibility, recognition, and inclusivity. It's a journey that redefines not just the workplace but the very essence of work itself.

Sustaining happiness over time in a workplace requires deliberate and ongoing efforts. It's not enough to create a burst of positivity; the challenge is to maintain it consistently. Key strategies to achieve this involve a blend of cultural, managerial, and policy-based approaches.

- Cultivating a culture of continuous recognition is essential. This means regularly acknowledging and celebrating both small wins and major achievements. Such recognition should come not only from the top but should also be encouraged among peers.

- Encouraging open and honest communication is crucial. Regular check-ins, town hall meetings, and feedback platforms can help maintain transparency and ensure that employees feel heard and valued. This open dialogue fosters trust and helps in addressing any issues before they escalate.

- Promoting work-life balance is a long-term commitment. This includes enforcing reasonable work hours, respecting boundaries, and encouraging employees to take their full vacation time. Flexible work arrangements can also contribute significantly to employee happiness.

- Investing in professional development demonstrates a commitment to employees' growth and satisfaction. Ongoing training opportunities, mentorship programs, and clear paths for advancement keep employees engaged and motivated.

- Prioritizing mental health and well-being is critical. This can be done through wellness programs, access to mental health resources, and a supportive environment where employees feel comfortable discussing their mental health without stigma.

- Fostering a sense of community and belonging within the workplace is also important. Team-building activities, social events, and community service projects can strengthen bonds among employees.

Leadership plays a key role in sustaining workplace happiness. Leaders who are empathetic, approachable, and lead by example in promoting a positive work culture can significantly influence the overall work environment. It's important to regularly assess the workplace atmosphere and employee satisfaction. Surveys, focus groups, and suggestion boxes can provide insights into the effectiveness of current strategies and highlight areas for improvement. By implementing these strategies, organizations can create a work environment where happiness is not just a fleeting moment but a sustained experience, leading to higher productivity, better employee retention, and overall organizational success.

In an ever-evolving business landscape, the ability to continuously refine and adapt processes, policies, and practices is crucial for long-term success and relevance. Continuous improvement fosters a culture of innovation and creativity, encouraging employees to constantly seek better ways to perform their tasks and solve problems. This mindset not only leads to increased efficiency and productivity but also keeps the organization ahead of the curve in a competitive market.

Adaptation is equally important. The ability to quickly respond to changes in the market, technology, or customer preferences is essential for survival and growth. Organizations that can pivot and adapt are better positioned to seize new opportunities and mitigate risks.

Moreover, continuous improvement and adaptation are key to employee engagement and satisfaction. A dynamic work environment where new ideas are valued, and change is embraced can be highly motivating for employees. It provides opportunities for learning and growth, which are important factors in job satisfaction and retention.

Incorporating feedback is a critical component of this process. Regularly soliciting and acting on feedback from employees, customers, and other stakeholders ensures that the organization remains responsive to their needs and expectations.

The commitment to continuous improvement and adaptation is essential for maintaining a competitive edge, fostering innovation, and ensuring employee satisfaction. It's a proactive approach that prepares organizations not just to respond to changes but to anticipate and capitalize on them.

Keeping up with changing employee needs and industry trends is a dynamic and ongoing process crucial for any organization's sustainability and growth. As the workforce evolves and industry landscapes shift, understanding and adapting to these changes is essential.

To keep pace with changing employee needs, organizations must regularly engage with their staff to understand their evolving expectations and preferences. This can be achieved through surveys, focus groups, and open forums. Staying attuned to employees' desires for flexible working arrangements, professional development opportunities, and work-life balance is key to retaining a motivated and satisfied workforce.

In terms of industry trends, staying informed requires a proactive approach. This involves monitoring market developments, technological advancements, and competitive strategies. Attending industry conferences, participating in professional networks, and encouraging continuous learning within the organization are effective ways to stay abreast of current trends.

Adapting to these changes often requires revisiting and revising company policies, strategies, and practices. This might involve updating training programs, revising benefits packages, or investing in new technologies to improve productivity and meet the evolving needs of the workforce.

Leadership plays a crucial role in this process. Leaders must be visionary, forward-thinking, and open to change. They should foster a culture of agility and innovation, where adapting to new trends and employee needs is part of the organizational ethos. Regularly reviewing and updating business strategies in response to industry trends is also vital. This ensures that the organization remains competitive and can capitalize on new opportunities.

Keeping up with changing employee needs and industry trends is about remaining flexible, responsive, and proactive. It's about creating an environment where change is embraced and where the organization is always ready to evolve to meet the demands of the modern workforce and market. This chapter has delved into a range of key concepts and strategies essential for creating and maintaining happy workplaces, an endeavor that is increasingly recognized as vital for organizational success. Central to this discussion has been the understanding that employee happiness is intrinsically linked to productivity, creativity, and overall job satisfaction.

The chapter began by defining what constitutes a 'Happy Workplace' – an environment that goes beyond basic job satisfaction to include genuine joy, fulfillment, and a sense of purpose in work. The significance of happiness in the workplace was underscored, highlighting its impact on both individual well-being and organizational performance.

To build such a workplace, the chapter explored various strategies.

1. Recognizing and addressing burnout and stress, particularly in high-pressure environments, through initiatives like wellness programs, flexible working arrangements, and supportive management.

2. Implementing programs and initiatives that promote overall well-being, including mental health support, professional development opportunities, and team-building activities.

3. Balancing the diverse needs and expectations of employees through flexible policies, inclusive practices, and a culture that values every individual's contribution.

4. The role of leadership in fostering a positive and inclusive environment was highlighted as crucial, emphasizing that leaders set the tone for the workplace culture.

5. The chapter also touched upon the importance of continuous improvement and adaptation, both in terms of responding to changing employee needs and keeping pace with industry trends.

6. Strategies for creating and sustaining a happy workplace over time were discussed, emphasizing the need for ongoing effort, commitment, and a strategic approach to employee engagement and satisfaction.

The chapter provided a comprehensive look at the various facets involved in creating a happy workplace. It presented a holistic approach that combines empathy, flexibility, inclusivity, and proactive management to foster an environment where employees can thrive and contribute to their fullest potential.

As we conclude this chapter on building workplace utopias, it's clear that the journey is both challenging and rewarding. Creating a utopia in the workplace goes beyond mere policy changes or the introduction of new programs; it requires a fundamental shift in how we perceive work and its role in our lives. This journey involves cultivating environments where respect, empathy, creativity, and collaboration are not just encouraged but are ingrained in the very fabric of the organizational culture.

The pursuit of a workplace utopia is not a static goal but a dynamic process of continuous growth and adaptation. It requires a commitment to understanding and responding to the evolving needs of employees, and to fostering a culture that celebrates diversity, encourages open communication, and prioritizes the well-being of each individual.

Leadership plays a pivotal role in this journey. Leaders who embody these values and demonstrate a genuine commitment to their employees' happiness set a powerful example. They create ripple effects that can transform entire organizations, making the workplace not just a place to work, but a place to grow, learn, and thrive.

The journey towards building workplace utopias is also about recognizing the interconnectedness of personal well-being and professional success. It's about understanding that when employees are happy, engaged, and fulfilled, they bring their best selves to work, driving innovation, productivity, and, ultimately, the success of the organization.

In closing, the journey towards creating happy workplaces is an ongoing endeavor, one that requires patience, commitment, and a deep understanding of the human aspects of work. It's a journey that challenges us to reimagine the workplace as a space of possibility, growth, and joy – a true utopia in the context of our modern world.

Chapter 11: "Sunshine Stories: When Good Prevails"

This chapter is an uplifting journey through a series of 'Sunshine Stories' – real-life narratives where positivity, ethical practices, and good leadership have triumphed in the business world. The intent is to provide readers with concrete examples of how principled behavior and a focus on the greater good can lead to successful and sustainable outcomes in various professional contexts.

The structure of the chapter is designed to be both informative and inspirational. It begins with an introduction to the concept of ethical leadership and its impact on organizations and society. This is followed by a collection of case studies and success stories from a range of industries, illustrating the powerful effects of integrity, social responsibility, and positivity in the workplace.

Each story is carefully chosen to highlight different aspects of good prevailing in the business world. These include narratives of companies turning around their fortunes through ethical practices, leaders making tough but principled decisions, and organizations implementing innovative, people-centered solutions to complex problems.

In addition to celebrating these successes, the chapter also delves into the strategies and mindsets behind them. It examines how companies can integrate ethical practices into their business models, how leaders can maintain integrity in challenging situations, and how positive workplace cultures can be nurtured and sustained.

The chapter concludes with reflections on the lessons learned from these stories and how they can inspire and guide individuals and organizations in their own pursuits of success and integrity.

The impact of positive leadership and ethical practices in the business world is both profound and far-reaching. When leaders prioritize integrity and positivity, it sets a powerful tone that resonates throughout the organization and extends to its various stakeholders.

Positive leadership fosters a culture of trust and respect within the organization. Employees who work under leaders who are ethical, transparent, and genuinely concerned about their well-being tend to be more engaged, motivated, and loyal. This type of leadership encourages an open and inclusive work environment where employees feel valued and empowered to contribute their best work.

Ethical practices in business are crucial for building and maintaining trust with customers and clients. In an era where consumers are increasingly conscious of corporate ethics, companies that demonstrate a commitment to ethical behavior can gain a significant competitive advantage. This can lead to increased customer loyalty, enhanced brand reputation, and ultimately, better financial performance.

In the broader context, positive leadership and ethical practices contribute to a more sustainable business model. Ethical companies often adopt long-term perspectives, considering the environmental and social impacts of their decisions. This approach not only helps in mitigating risks but also opens up opportunities for innovation and growth in areas like sustainable development and corporate social responsibility.

Ethical business practices play a critical role in attracting and retaining top talent. Today's workforce, especially the younger generation, seeks more than just a paycheck; they are looking for employers whose values align with their own. Companies known for their ethical practices and positive work environments are more likely to attract these employees.

In the financial landscape, ethical behavior can also lead to more stable and profitable investment opportunities. Investors are increasingly looking towards companies with strong ethical foundations for long-term investments, as these companies are perceived to be less risky and more capable of sustained growth.

The impact of positive leadership and ethical practices in the business world goes beyond just creating a pleasant work environment. It drives employee satisfaction, customer loyalty, brand reputation, sustainable growth, and long-term financial success, making it an essential strategy for any forward-thinking business.

In defining 'good' in the context of business, it's crucial to look beyond the traditional metrics of success such as profitability and growth and consider the ethical dimensions of business practices and leadership. 'Good' in business encapsulates a spectrum of practices and values. It includes adhering to ethical standards, demonstrating social responsibility, ensuring fairness and integrity in dealings, and making decisions that consider the well-being of employees, customers, and the broader community. It's about conducting business in a way that is not only profitable but also just and sustainable.

The balance between profitability and ethical practices is a key aspect of this discussion. While profitability is essential for any business's survival and growth, how this profit is made matters greatly. 'Good' businesses understand that long-term success is deeply intertwined with ethical practices. They recognize that unethical behavior, while it may offer short-term gains, can lead to long-term risks, including damage to reputation, legal penalties, and loss of trust among stakeholders.

Good leadership is instrumental in cultivating and maintaining this balance. Leaders who prioritize ethical practices and create a culture of integrity set the stage for the entire organization. They influence the organizational culture by embedding ethical values into the core business strategy and decision-making processes. This kind of leadership fosters an environment where employees feel respected and valued, leading to higher levels of engagement, loyalty, and productivity. This kind of leadership in business extends to how companies treat their employees, customers, and the environment. It involves creating inclusive workplaces, providing fair and equal opportunities, engaging in fair trade practices, and adopting eco-friendly policies.

'Good' in business is about aligning financial objectives with ethical values. It's about leading with integrity and creating value not just for shareholders, but for all stakeholders, including employees, customers, communities, and the environment. This comprehensive approach to business practices and leadership not only enhances the company's reputation and sustainability but also contributes to the greater good of society.

The business landscape is dotted with narratives of companies that have boldly chosen ethics over short-term gains, often facing significant challenges but emerging stronger and more respected. These stories serve as testaments to the value of integrity and principled leadership in the corporate world.

One such narrative revolves around a consumer goods company that decided to source its raw materials ethically, even though it meant a considerable increase in costs. Initially, this decision put the company at a competitive disadvantage, as their products became more expensive than those of competitors who sourced cheaper, less ethically produced materials. However, by transparently communicating their commitment to ethical sourcing to their customers, the company not only retained its loyal customer base but also attracted a new segment of socially conscious consumers. In the long run, this decision bolstered the company's reputation and led to sustainable growth.

Another example comes from a tech company that refused to compromise on customer privacy, despite pressure to monetize user data. This stance led to initial financial setbacks and criticism from investors seeking quicker returns. The leadership, however, remained steadfast in their commitment to user privacy. Over time, as public concern over data privacy grew, the company's steadfast approach earned them widespread trust and loyalty, setting them apart in an industry often criticized for exploiting user data. Their commitment to ethical practices eventually translated into long-term profitability and industry leadership.

A financial services firm also stands out in its decision to implement stringent compliance and transparency policies, even when such measures seemed excessive compared to industry norms. This move initially resulted in slower processes and lost opportunities where speed was essential. However, when the industry faced a series of scandals and regulatory crackdowns, this firm emerged unscathed, with its reputation for integrity intact. Their foresight and commitment to ethical practices paid off, attracting clients who valued transparency and long-term stability.

In each of these stories, the common challenges faced by the businesses were financial pressures, competitive disadvantages, and skepticism from stakeholders accustomed to conventional business practices. Overcoming these challenges required a combination of strong leadership, clear communication of their ethical principles to their stakeholders, and a long-term vision that prioritized sustainable success over immediate gains.

These narratives highlight that while the path of prioritizing ethics over short-term gains is fraught with challenges, it can lead to enduring success, respect, and a legacy that transcends financial achievements. These companies not only reaped the benefits in terms of profitability and growth but also set new standards in their respective industries, inspiring a broader movement towards ethical business practices.

The long-term benefits realized from ethical decisions in business are both tangible and intangible, contributing to the overall health and sustainability of a company. While the immediate gains of ethical practices might not always be evident, their impact over time can be profound and far-reaching.

1. Enhanced Reputation and Brand Loyalty: Ethical decisions help build a strong, positive reputation for a company. This reputation for integrity attracts customers and clients who value and prioritize doing business with ethically responsible

companies. Over time, this can lead to increased brand loyalty and a more dedicated customer base.

2. Attracting and Retaining Talent: Companies known for their ethical practices are more attractive to top talent. Employees today are looking for more than just a paycheck; they seek employers whose values align with their own. Ethical companies tend to have higher employee satisfaction, lower turnover rates, and are able to attract talent who are committed to the company's mission.

3. Long-Term Financial Performance: Ethical decisions often lead to sustainable financial performance. While unethical practices might yield short-term profits, they come with high risks including legal penalties and lost trust. Ethical companies avoid these risks and are more likely to enjoy long-term financial stability and profitability.

4. Investor Attraction: Ethical behavior and sustainable practices are increasingly important to investors. Ethically sound companies are often viewed as less risky and more capable of sustained growth, attracting investors who are looking for long-term, stable returns.

5. Regulatory Compliance: Ethical decisions help companies stay compliant with laws and regulations. This compliance not only avoids legal penalties and fines but also reduces the risk of reputational damage associated with legal issues.

6. Improved Risk Management: Ethical practices lead to better risk management. Companies that operate ethically are less likely to face scandals, boycotts, or public backlash, which can be costly and damaging.

7. Creating Positive Social Impact: Ethical decisions often contribute to positive social change. Companies that prioritize ethics can influence industry standards, inspire other companies to follow suit, and contribute positively to the communities in which they operate.

8. Employee Morale and Productivity: Working for an ethical company boosts employee morale and productivity. Employees are more engaged and motivated when they feel they are part of an organization that does good and values its people.

Real-life examples of leaders who are renowned for their positive influence and ethical leadership span various industries and sectors. These leaders have not only made a significant impact on their organizations but have also left a lasting legacy in their respective fields.

- Satya Nadella, CEO of Microsoft: Since taking the helm in 2014, Nadella has been credited with transforming Microsoft's culture and business. He shifted the company's focus from competition to innovation and collaboration, emphasizing empathy as a core value in decision-making. His leadership style is inclusive and growth-oriented, focusing on continuous learning and development. Under his leadership, Microsoft has seen a resurgence in relevance and profitability, fostering a culture of innovation and ethical responsibility.

- Indra Nooyi, former CEO of PepsiCo: Nooyi is celebrated for redefining PepsiCo's business strategy with a focus on health and sustainability. She pioneered the "Performance with Purpose" initiative, aligning profit with societal contributions. Her decision-making process involved long-term planning and consideration of environmental and social impacts. Nooyi's legacy includes transforming PepsiCo into a more sustainable and socially responsible company while delivering strong financial performance.

- Paul Polman, former CEO of Unilever: Polman is known for his commitment to sustainable business practices. He made a bold decision to prioritize long-term sustainability goals over short-term profit pressures. His leadership style is characterized by a focus on collective well-being and environmental stewardship. Under Polman, Unilever set ambitious sustainability targets, influencing other companies to follow suit, and proving that ethical business practices can drive success.

- Howard Schultz, former CEO of Starbucks: Schultz's leadership at Starbucks was marked by a strong commitment to employee welfare and corporate social responsibility. He introduced employee benefits like health insurance, stock options, and tuition reimbursement, even for part-time workers. Schultz's decision-making emphasized ethical considerations and community involvement, helping to build Starbucks into a globally respected brand known for its positive corporate culture.

- Shantanu Narayen, CEO of Adobe: Narayen has led Adobe through a successful business transformation, focusing on innovation and customer experience. His leadership style is collaborative and forward-thinking, emphasizing the importance of creativity and diversity in the workplace. Under his guidance, Adobe has been recognized for its ethical business practices, inclusive culture, and sustainable growth.

These leaders stand out for their ethical leadership styles and decision-making processes that consider the broader impact on society and the environment. They have created legacies that go beyond financial success, including fostering inclusive and sustainable business cultures, promoting social responsibility, and influencing positive changes in their industries. Their examples demonstrate how ethical and positive leadership can lead to significant and enduring organizational success.

In the realm of modern business, the implementation of transformative policies and practices stands as a testament to the power of progressive leadership. These initiatives, often pioneering and bold, have demonstrated significant positive impacts, not only within the organizations that adopt them but also across their respective industries.

One striking example of such transformative policies is the adoption of flexible working arrangements. This approach, which gained momentum in response to evolving workforce demands and technological advancements, has redefined the traditional work environment. Companies that have embraced flexible working schedules and remote working options have reported a surge in employee productivity, satisfaction, and loyalty. The implementation of these policies typically involved a reassessment of work norms, substantial investment in digital infrastructure, and a shift towards a results-oriented culture. Employees and stakeholders welcomed these changes, appreciating the greater work-life balance and the trust placed in them by the organization.

Another example is the focus on environmental sustainability. Companies across various sectors have integrated green practices into their operations, ranging from reducing carbon footprints to adopting renewable energy sources. The implementation of these practices often required a complete overhaul of existing processes, significant investment, and a long-term commitment to sustainability goals. The response from employees and stakeholders has been overwhelmingly positive, with an increase in employee engagement and a stronger brand reputation. Consumers, in particular, have shown a preference for brands that demonstrate environmental responsibility, leading to increased customer loyalty and market share.

The ripple effect of such transformative policies in the industry has been profound. Organizations that have taken the lead in implementing flexible work arrangements or sustainability initiatives have set new benchmarks, prompting competitors and industry peers to follow suit. This domino effect has led to widespread changes across industries, elevating standards and expectations for workplace flexibility, environmental responsibility, and ethical business practices.

These transformative policies and practices illustrate the significant impact that innovative and ethical leadership can have. By prioritizing employee well-being, environmental sustainability, and stakeholder engagement, businesses are not only enhancing their performance and reputation but also contributing to a broader movement towards a more sustainable and equitable future in the business world.

Another notable case study involves a leading financial institution faced with a significant ethical dilemma involving consumer data privacy. The company discovered a vulnerability that potentially compromised client information. Rather than concealing the issue to avoid backlash, the firm chose transparency. They promptly informed affected customers and invested in robust cybersecurity measures to prevent future breaches. This decision, while initially leading to short-term reputational damage, eventually strengthened client trust due to the company's commitment to integrity and transparency.

A further case revolves around a multinational manufacturing company grappling with labor practices in its overseas factories. Reports of poor working conditions and low wages surfaced, putting the company at a crossroads. Choosing to prioritize ethical labor practices, they overhauled their supply chain management, set higher standards for working conditions, and implemented regular audits to ensure compliance. This move not only improved conditions for thousands of workers but also enhanced the company's brand reputation and consumer trust.

A technology giant faced a different kind of ethical challenge when it came to market competition. The company was accused of engaging in anti-competitive practices. In response, instead of embarking on lengthy legal battles, the company chose to review and modify its business practices, ensuring fair competition. This decision fostered a more competitive market and ultimately led to more innovation in the industry.

From these experiences, several lessons emerge. Firstly, upholding integrity may pose short-term challenges but often leads to long-term gains in trust and reputation. Secondly, ethical dilemmas should be approached with transparency and a willingness to make necessary changes, even if they require significant investment or a radical shift in operations. Finally, a commitment to ethical practices is not just about adhering to legal standards but also about setting a higher bar for corporate responsibility.

These case studies exemplify how companies can successfully overcome adversity by adhering to principles of integrity. They illustrate that ethical business practices are not just a moral obligation but a strategic imperative that can lead to sustainable success and a positive corporate legacy.

An examination of Corporate Social Responsibility (CSR) initiatives and their impact reveals a multi-faceted approach where businesses extend their responsibilities beyond shareholders to include wider societal interests. This strategic integration of social and environmental concerns in business operations has far-reaching implications, yielding long-term benefits for both businesses and communities.

CSR initiatives vary widely, ranging from environmental sustainability efforts, such as reducing carbon footprints and embracing renewable energy, to social endeavors like community development projects, philanthropy, and ethical labor practices. A notable example is a global technology company that invested heavily in renewable energy for its data centers, significantly reducing its environmental impact. Another instance is a retail giant launching extensive community development programs, focusing on education and healthcare in underprivileged areas.

The implementation of these initiatives often requires substantial resource allocation, strategic planning, and a shift in corporate philosophy. However, the impacts are profound and multifaceted. Environmentally focused CSR initiatives, for example, help in conserving natural resources, reducing pollution, and combating climate change. Socially oriented programs contribute to community development, enhance the quality of life for individuals, and address societal challenges like poverty and inequality.

From a business perspective, effective CSR strategies lead to numerous long-term benefits. They enhance brand reputation and customer loyalty, as consumers increasingly prefer brands with strong social and environmental credentials. CSR also contributes to employee satisfaction and morale; employees tend to feel more engaged and motivated when working for a company that demonstrates a commitment to societal and environmental causes. CSR initiatives can open up new market opportunities and drive innovation. For instance, sustainable business practices can lead to the development of new, eco-friendly products or services, tapping into a growing market of environmentally conscious consumers.

For communities, the benefits of CSR are tangible. Sustainable business practices lead to healthier ecosystems and a cleaner environment, while social initiatives contribute to improved education, healthcare, and overall community well-being. These efforts can stimulate local economies and create job opportunities, leading to a positive cycle of growth and development. CSR initiatives represent a significant shift in how businesses view and execute their role in society. Far from being a mere corporate obligation, these initiatives have evolved into a strategic business imperative that delivers substantial benefits to companies and communities alike. By embracing CSR, businesses not only contribute to a more sustainable and equitable world but also position themselves for long-term success and growth.

The stories and case studies in this chapter offer a wealth of insights and key takeaways for future leaders aiming to implement ethical and positive leadership practices in various organizational contexts. These narratives are not just inspirational; they provide a practical blueprint for driving meaningful change and fostering a culture of integrity and responsibility.

One of the primary takeaways from this chapter is the importance of aligning business practices with ethical standards and societal values. Future leaders are encouraged to look beyond profit margins and consider the broader impact of their decisions on employees, communities, and the environment. This involves adopting a long-term perspective, focusing on sustainable growth rather than short-term gains.

To implement similar practices, leaders should start by establishing a clear vision and set of values that reflect their commitment to ethical and positive leadership. This vision should be communicated effectively across the organization, ensuring that all employees understand and are aligned with these values. It's crucial to embed these principles into the company's operations, from decision-making processes to daily business practices.

Building a culture of transparency and trust is essential. Leaders should encourage open communication, foster an environment where employees feel safe to voice their opinions and concerns, and ensure that there is a consistent and fair approach to addressing these issues. Another key aspect is the integration of CSR initiatives into the business strategy. This could involve environmental sustainability programs, community engagement projects, or initiatives focused on employee well-being. These efforts should not be seen as ancillary but as integral to the company's core operations.

Leaders are also encouraged to lead by example, demonstrating the values they wish to instill in their organization. Ethical leadership is as much about personal conduct as it is about organizational policies. Leaders should exhibit the behaviors and attitudes they expect from their teams, showing commitment to ethical practices in their actions. Additionally, future leaders should be adaptable and open to learning. The landscape of business and societal expectations is constantly evolving, and leaders need to be prepared to adjust their strategies and approaches in response to these changes.

In terms of encouragement, future leaders are reminded that pursuing ethical and positive leadership is not just the right thing to do morally, but it also makes sound business sense. Companies led by ethical leaders tend to have better reputations, more engaged employees, and stronger customer loyalty, all of which contribute to long-term success. The chapter serves as a call to action for future leaders to embrace ethical and positive leadership. By doing so, they can drive their organizations towards success while contributing to a more equitable and sustainable world.

The chapter on the power of good in business leadership compellingly underscores the profound impact that ethical and positive leadership can have on organizations and society at large. It serves as a testament to the transformative potential of leadership that is rooted in integrity, empathy, and a commitment to the greater good.

Throughout the chapter, the recurring theme is the undeniable influence of ethical leadership practices in shaping the culture, reputation, and success of an organization. It illustrates through various examples how leaders who prioritize ethical considerations, social responsibility, and employee well-being not only cultivate a positive and productive workplace but also contribute to the broader societal good. These leaders set a powerful precedent, demonstrating that ethical behavior and business success are not mutually exclusive but rather, mutually reinforcing.

Reflecting on the potential for positive change in the business world, the chapter highlights the shifting paradigm where businesses are increasingly seen as key players in addressing global challenges. From sustainability initiatives to fair labor practices and community engagement, the role of businesses in fostering social and environmental progress is more critical than ever. The chapter posits that leaders who embrace this broader vision of business responsibility can drive significant and lasting change, benefitting both their organizations and the world.

In its closing thoughts, the chapter emphasizes the importance of integrity and ethical practices in shaping a better future. It asserts that the values and principles at the heart of an organization are the guiding forces that determine its impact and legacy. Leaders who operate with honesty, transparency, and a commitment to doing what is right pave the way for a future where businesses are a force for positive change. They inspire trust and loyalty among stakeholders, foster a culture of respect and collaboration within their organizations, and contribute to building a more equitable and sustainable society.

This chapter serves as both a reflection on the transformative power of ethical leadership and a call to action for current and future leaders. It encourages them to embrace a leadership ethos that prioritizes integrity and social responsibility, reminding them that their decisions and actions have the power to shape not just the future of their organizations but also the future of our global community.

Chapter 12: "The Path to Enlightenment: How to Be a Light Leader"

We now embark on a profound journey, exploring the transformative process of becoming a Light Leader. Having previously defined the essence of Light Leadership, this chapter shifts focus to the dynamic and insightful journey towards achieving this revered leadership style. The chapter begins by setting the stage for what it means to embark on the path to Light Leadership. It presents an overview of the journey, which is not just a professional endeavor but also a deeply personal one. This journey involves introspection, learning, and a commitment to embodying the principles of empathy, transparency, and a focus on collective well-being – the hallmarks of Light Leadership.

As the chapter unfolds, it delves into the various stages of this journey. It starts with self-awareness, highlighting the importance of understanding one's values, strengths, and areas for growth. The narrative then guides the reader through the process of cultivating key skills and attributes essential for a Light Leader, such as emotional intelligence, effective communication, and ethical decision-making. Additionally, the chapter explores strategies for implementing Light Leadership principles in various organizational contexts. It provides practical advice on fostering a positive and inclusive work environment, encouraging innovation, and leading with compassion and integrity.

The chapter is structured to provide a comprehensive guide for aspiring Light Leaders, combining theoretical insights with practical strategies and real-life examples. It aims to inspire and equip readers with the tools and understanding necessary to embark on this rewarding leadership path.

"The Path to Enlightenment: How to Be a Light Leader" serves as a roadmap for those aspiring to transform not only their leadership style but also the culture and performance of their organizations. It encourages leaders to pursue a path of continuous growth and learning, ultimately leading to a more fulfilling and impactful leadership journey.

Light Leadership, as a concept, is deeply rooted in both psychological and philosophical principles, offering a holistic approach to leadership that transcends traditional methods. This leadership style is predicated on the belief that effective leadership is not just about driving results but also about nurturing the growth and well-being of both individuals and organizations. The in-depth explanation of Light Leadership principles, along with their psychological and philosophical underpinnings, reveals a multifaceted approach to leading in the modern world.

- Empathy: At the heart of Light Leadership lies the principle of empathy. Psychologically, empathy involves the ability to understand and share the feelings of others. It's about seeing the world through others' eyes and responding with compassion and understanding. Philosophically, empathy is grounded in the concept of interconnectedness – the idea that all individuals are part of a larger whole and that understanding this connection is crucial for effective leadership. Empathetic leaders are adept at building strong, trusting relationships, fostering a collaborative and supportive work environment.

- Transparency: Transparency in Light Leadership is about openness and honesty in all aspects of leadership. Psychologically, transparency builds trust and security within an organization, as employees feel more valued and respected when they are informed and included in decision-making processes. From a philosophical perspective, transparency is linked to the concept of authenticity – the idea that leaders should be true to their values and transparent about their intentions and actions. This principle encourages a culture of honesty and integrity, where ethical behavior is not just encouraged but expected.

- Collective Well-Being: This principle is focused on the overall health and happiness of the team and organization. Psychologically, this speaks to the human need for belonging and significance. Leaders who prioritize collective well-being understand that employees are more motivated and productive when they feel part of a supportive community. Philosophically, this principle is rooted in utilitarianism – the idea that the best action is the one that maximizes utility, generally defined as that which produces the greatest well-being of the greatest number of people. This principle fosters a culture of care and concern for the well-being of all stakeholders.

- Inclusivity: Inclusivity in Light Leadership involves valuing diversity and ensuring everyone has a voice. Psychologically, inclusivity meets the basic human need for belonging and respect. Diverse perspectives are not only acknowledged but celebrated. Philosophically, inclusivity is grounded in egalitarianism – the belief in the equality of all people. Leaders who practice inclusivity create environments where differences are seen as strengths, leading to more innovative and effective problem-solving.

- Sustainability: Light Leadership also emphasizes sustainability, both in environmental and business practices. Psychologically, this principle reflects a long-term perspective, considering the future impact of today's actions. Philosophically, it is rooted in the principle of stewardship – the responsible management of resources, including people, finances, and the environment. Sustainable leadership practices ensure the longevity and health of both the organization and the planet.

Light Leadership is a forward-thinking, human-centric approach. It integrates psychological understanding with deep philosophical insights, offering a more comprehensive and empathetic way of leading. It encourages leaders to go beyond traditional metrics of success, focusing instead on creating an environment where employees feel valued, ethics are prioritized, and the organization contributes positively to society.

Light Leadership stands in marked contrast to traditional leadership models, offering a distinctive approach that reflects the evolving needs and values of modern organizations and their employees. This contrast can be understood through several key dimensions:

1. Focus on Empathy vs. Authority: Traditional leadership models often emphasize authority and control, with leaders making decisions based on hierarchical structures and positional power. Light Leadership, conversely, focuses on empathy and understanding. It values emotional intelligence and the ability to connect with and understand the needs and motivations of team members, fostering a more inclusive and supportive work environment.

2. Transparency and Openness vs. Top-Down Decision Making: In traditional leadership, decisions are frequently made at the top and then communicated down the chain of command, often with limited explanation or input from lower levels. Light Leadership advocates for transparency and openness, involving team members in decision-making processes and ensuring that actions and intentions are communicated clearly and honestly.

3. Collective Well-Being vs. Individual Performance: Traditional models tend to focus on individual performance and competition, sometimes at the expense of team harmony and collaboration. Light Leadership, in contrast, emphasizes collective well-being and the success of the team as a whole. It recognizes that a supportive and collaborative work culture can lead to better outcomes for the organization and its members.

4. Inclusivity vs. Exclusivity: Traditional leadership often values uniformity and may inadvertently marginalize diverse

perspectives. Light Leadership, however, actively seeks out and values diversity, understanding that a variety of perspectives can lead to more innovative solutions and a more dynamic workplace.

5. Sustainability and Long-term Thinking vs. Short-term Gains: Traditional leadership models are often driven by short-term goals and immediate results, sometimes at the expense of long-term sustainability. Light Leadership takes a broader view, considering the long-term impact of decisions on people, the organization, and the environment.

6. Ethical Consideration vs. Profit Maximization: While traditional leadership models are typically centered around maximizing profits and shareholder value, Light Leadership places a strong emphasis on ethics and social responsibility. It advocates for doing what is right, not just what is profitable, believing that ethical business practices lead to sustainable success.

Light Leadership represents a paradigm shift from traditional leadership models. It moves away from hierarchical, authoritative, and profit-centric approaches, towards a more empathetic, inclusive, and ethically driven style. This approach aligns with contemporary workforce expectations and the growing emphasis on social and environmental responsibility in the business world.

Self-assessment and awareness are critical components of Light Leadership, as they provide leaders with insights into their own strengths, weaknesses, and areas for growth. Developing a deep understanding of oneself is essential for embodying the principles of empathy, transparency, and inclusivity that are central to this leadership style. One effective method for self-assessment in leadership is reflective practice. This involves regularly taking time to reflect on one's actions, decisions, and their outcomes. Leaders can keep a journal to document their experiences, thoughts, and feelings about their leadership journey. Reflective practice encourages introspection and helps leaders identify patterns in their behavior and areas where they can improve.

Another valuable tool for self-assessment is feedback from others. Leaders can seek constructive feedback from their peers, superiors, and team members. This feedback provides external perspectives on a leader's style and effectiveness. Conducting 360-degree feedback sessions, where leaders receive anonymous feedback from a range of people they work with, can be particularly insightful.

Personality and behavioral assessments are also beneficial for self-awareness. Tools like the Myers-Briggs Type Indicator (MBTI), the Big Five Personality Traits, or the DISC Assessment can help leaders understand their inherent personality traits and how these traits influence their leadership style. Emotional intelligence assessments are particularly relevant for Light Leadership. Tools like the Emotional Intelligence Appraisal or the Bar-On Emotional Quotient Inventory (EQ-i) can help leaders gauge their emotional intelligence, which is crucial for developing empathy and building strong relationships.

Mindfulness practices also play a crucial role in developing self-awareness. Regular mindfulness exercises, such as meditation or focused breathing, can help leaders become more aware of their thoughts and emotions, leading to greater self-control and a better ability to respond to situations calmly and empathetically. Seeking mentorship or coaching can aid in self-assessment. Experienced mentors or coaches can provide valuable insights, challenge leaders to look at things from different perspectives, and guide them in their personal and professional development.

Light Leadership requires a commitment to ongoing self-assessment and awareness. By regularly engaging in these practices, leaders can develop a deeper understanding of themselves, which is essential for leading others effectively and authentically.

Understanding one's strengths and areas for improvement, coupled with heightened self-awareness, is pivotal in the realm of effective leadership, particularly within the framework of Light Leadership. This self-understanding not only enhances a leader's ability to manage and inspire their teams but also fosters personal growth and development.

Recognizing one's strengths allows a leader to leverage these attributes effectively. For instance, a leader with strong communication skills can be adept at conveying vision and motivating the team, while one with great analytical abilities can excel in strategic planning and problem-solving. Utilizing these strengths in the right contexts amplifies a leader's effectiveness and sets a positive example for the team.

Conversely, being aware of areas for improvement is equally crucial. It involves acknowledging weaknesses or gaps in one's leadership style and taking proactive steps to address them. For example, a leader who struggles with delegation might work on trusting team members more and refining their approach to task allocation. Acknowledging and working on these areas not only leads to personal growth but also demonstrates a commitment to self-improvement, a quality that is inspiring and motivating for team members.

The importance of self-awareness in effective leadership cannot be overstated. Self-aware leaders are more likely to act with intention, make informed decisions, and adapt their style to suit different situations. They are also better equipped to manage their emotions and responses, a key aspect of emotional intelligence, which in turn influences their interactions with others. This self-awareness fosters a more authentic leadership style, as leaders who are in tune with their strengths and weaknesses are more genuine in their actions and interactions.

Self-aware leaders are typically more empathetic and understanding, as they can relate their experiences to those of their team members. This empathy is a cornerstone of Light Leadership, as it fosters a supportive and inclusive environment, encouraging open communication and collaboration. Understanding one's strengths and areas for improvement through self-awareness is a fundamental aspect of Light Leadership. It not only enhances a leader's effectiveness and credibility but also contributes to a positive organizational culture, where growth, learning, and empathy are valued and encouraged.

Developing core Light Leadership qualities such as empathy, transparency, and a focus on collective well-being is a journey that intertwines self-awareness with consistent practice and dedication to personal growth. This development involves a combination of reflective exercises, open communication, and fostering a supportive team environment.

Cultivating empathy starts with active listening. This means fully focusing on the speaker during conversations, understanding their perspective, and responding thoughtfully. Enhancing empathy also involves empathy exercises like role-reversal, where you try to see situations from your team members' viewpoints. Regular team meetings or one-on-one sessions can facilitate this. Additionally, reflecting on your daily interactions each evening, and considering moments where greater empathy could have been exhibited, can also be beneficial.

Fostering transparency involves openly sharing your thought processes and decisions with your team. This not only includes explaining the reasoning behind your actions but also being candid about challenges and uncertainties. Building a culture where honest feedback is encouraged and valued is crucial. This involves creating a safe space where team members can share their thoughts freely. Daily check-ins, whether through meetings or digital communication, keep everyone informed and involved, reinforcing this transparent culture.

A focus on collective well-being can be nurtured through regular team-building activities that strengthen relationships and foster a sense of community. Implementing well-being initiatives like wellness programs and stress management workshops demonstrates a commitment to the team's overall health. Regular recognition and appreciation of team members' efforts and achievements also contribute significantly to a positive and supportive work environment.

Incorporating mindfulness practices into your daily routine enhances focus and presence, which are vital for empathetic and transparent leadership. Continuous learning about different leadership styles and emotional intelligence broadens your understanding and effectiveness as a leader. Finally, regular self-reflection is essential to assess your growth in these areas and identify aspects that need more attention.

Stories and examples of empathy, transparency, and a focus on collective well-being in action illustrate how these core Light Leadership qualities can transform leadership practices and organizational culture.

Empathy in Action

A tech company CEO faced significant backlash after a product failure. Instead of deflecting blame, she empathetically acknowledged the team's hard work and the disappointment they all felt. She organized open forums for employees to express their concerns and suggestions. This approach not only soothed frayed nerves but also fostered a culture of mutual support and resilience, leading to a successful product revival.

Transparency in Action

The leader of a non-profit organization had to make budget cuts due to funding reductions. Understanding the potential impact on staff morale, he held a series of open meetings to discuss the organization's financial state. He transparently shared the challenges and involved the team in brainstorming cost-saving strategies. This open approach not only eased anxieties but also led to innovative solutions that minimized the impact on the staff and the organization's mission.

Collective Well-being in Action

A manufacturing plant manager noticed a gradual decline in employee morale and productivity. Recognizing the need to prioritize collective well-being, she initiated a series of workshops focused on team-building and stress management. Additionally, she introduced flexible working hours to improve work-life balance. These measures resulted in a noticeable improvement in team cohesion, job satisfaction, and productivity.

Combined Qualities in Action

A school principal was tasked with turning around a school struggling with low student achievement and staff turnover. She started with empathetic one-on-one conversations with teachers to understand their challenges and needs. With a commitment to transparency, she shared her vision and the realistic challenges ahead, ensuring her plans and decisions were openly communicated and feedback was encouraged. She also prioritized collective well-being by implementing collaborative teaching strategies and professional development opportunities. This holistic approach led to improved teacher morale, higher student engagement, and academic performance.

These stories exemplify how empathy, transparency, and a focus on collective well-being can create positive outcomes in various organizational contexts. Light Leadership, as shown through these examples, has the power to create environments where trust, collaboration, and a shared sense of purpose thrive, leading to enhanced organizational performance and a positive work culture.

Effective, empathetic communication is a cornerstone of Light Leadership, playing a crucial role in building trust and strong relationships within a team. This style of communication is characterized by its focus on understanding and addressing the needs, feelings, and perspectives of others, while also clearly expressing one's own thoughts and intentions.

To practice empathetic communication, start by actively listening to your team members. This means giving them your full attention, acknowledging their feelings, and responding in a way that shows you truly understand their perspective. It's about more than just hearing the words; it's about grasping the emotions and intentions behind them.

Asking open-ended questions is another effective technique. This encourages dialogue and shows your team that you value their input and are interested in their viewpoints. It helps to foster a more inclusive and collaborative environment where everyone feels comfortable sharing their ideas and concerns.

Non-verbal cues are also an essential aspect of empathetic communication. Maintaining eye contact, using appropriate body language, and being mindful of your tone of voice can greatly enhance the way your message is received. These non-verbal signals can convey respect, attentiveness, and understanding, reinforcing the verbal message.

When communicating, especially in challenging situations, it's important to express yourself clearly and honestly, while also being sensitive to how your words might affect others. This balance ensures that your message is conveyed with integrity and consideration.

Building trust and strong relationships within a team requires consistency and reliability. Trust is fostered when leaders follow through on their promises, show consistency in their actions and decisions, and treat all team members fairly and with respect.

Creating an environment of psychological safety is also key. When team members feel safe to take risks, voice their opinions, and express their true selves without fear of negative consequences, it strengthens trust and encourages open communication.

Recognizing and celebrating achievements, both at an individual and team level, also helps in building strong relationships. Acknowledging hard work and successes makes team members feel valued and appreciated, which in turn fosters loyalty and a strong sense of team spirit.

Investing time in getting to know your team members on a personal level can go a long way in building strong relationships. Understanding their interests, motivations, and career aspirations shows that you care about them not just as employees but as individuals, which is a fundamental aspect of Light Leadership.

Effective, empathetic communication coupled with actions that build trust and demonstrate care and respect, lay the foundation for strong, healthy relationships within a team. This approach not only enhances team cohesion and morale but also drives better collaboration and overall organizational success.

Case studies on successful communication strategies in leadership provide real-world examples of how effective communication can enhance leadership effectiveness and improve organizational outcomes.

Case Study 1: Tech Company Turnaround

A tech company was struggling with low employee morale and high turnover. The new CEO implemented an open-door policy, encouraging employees at all levels to share their ideas and concerns directly with her. She also initiated regular town hall meetings where she transparently discussed company challenges and successes. These communication strategies led to a significant increase in employee trust and engagement, a decrease in turnover, and a surge in innovation and productivity.

Case Study 2: Healthcare Organization's Response to Crisis

During a healthcare crisis, a hospital's leadership team faced immense pressure and uncertainty. The CEO held daily briefings with staff, providing updates on the situation and the hospital's response. She made a point to acknowledge the hard work and dedication of her staff and to express empathy for the challenges they faced. Her honest and compassionate communication fostered a sense of unity and resilience among the staff, leading to improved patient care and staff well-being during a critical time.

Case Study 3: Retail Chain's Cultural Shift

A national retail chain implemented a new strategy focused on improving employee engagement and customer service. The leadership team conducted a series of workshops and training sessions to improve internal communication skills. Managers were trained in active listening, giving constructive feedback, and resolving conflicts effectively. This focus on communication led to a more positive work environment, higher employee satisfaction, and improved customer service ratings.

Case Study 4: Global Corporation's Cross-Cultural Communication

In a global corporation with a diverse workforce, the leadership recognized the need for better cross-cultural communication. They introduced cultural competency training for all employees and established a diversity council to address communication barriers. The company also implemented language translation tools and cultural exchange programs. These efforts improved understanding and collaboration across different regions and cultures, leading to more effective global teamwork and enhanced business performance.

These case studies illustrate how successful communication strategies in leadership can lead to improved employee engagement, better crisis management, a more positive organizational culture, and effective cross-cultural collaboration. They demonstrate that clear, empathetic, and inclusive communication is a powerful tool in a leader's repertoire, capable of transforming organizational dynamics and driving success.

Creating a vision and inspiring others is a critical aspect of leadership, involving the art of crafting a compelling vision for the future and the ability to motivate and engage team members to work towards that vision.

The process of crafting a compelling vision starts with a deep understanding of the organization's purpose and values. A leader must reflect on what makes their organization unique and how it can make a difference. This vision should be forward-looking, painting a picture of what the future could look like if the organization achieves its goals. It needs to be ambitious enough to inspire, but also realistic enough to be achievable.

A key to making a vision compelling is to connect it with the values and aspirations of the team members. It should resonate on a personal level, making each member feel that they are contributing to something larger than themselves. This involves communicating the vision in a way that is relatable and stirs emotion, making it not just an organizational goal, but a shared dream.

Inspiring and motivating team members requires more than just a well-articulated vision; it requires a leader to embody that vision in their daily actions and decisions. A leader must be the champion of the vision, consistently reinforcing it and demonstrating commitment through their actions. This consistency builds trust and credibility, making it easier for team members to buy into and commit to the vision.

Another technique for inspiring team members is to empower them. This involves giving them the autonomy to make decisions and take actions that align with the vision. Empowerment fosters a sense of ownership and responsibility, which can be highly motivating. It also involves providing the necessary resources, support, and training to enable team members to contribute effectively to the vision.

Recognition and appreciation play a crucial role in motivation. Acknowledging individual and team achievements that contribute to the vision reinforces positive behaviors and encourages continued effort. Celebrating milestones and successes along the way keeps the team motivated and focused.

A leader must be an effective communicator, able to articulate the vision in a way that is clear, compelling, and inspiring. This involves tailoring the message to different audiences and finding ways to keep the vision front and center in the organization's day-to-day activities.

Creating a vision and inspiring others is about connecting the future goals of the organization with the values and aspirations of its people. It requires a leader to be both a visionary and a motivator, able to paint a picture of a compelling future and engage their team in making that future a reality.

Examples of visionary Light Leaders demonstrate how impactful leadership, guided by principles of empathy, transparency, and collective well-being, can lead to remarkable achievements and positive change within organizations and communities.

Satya Nadella, CEO of Microsoft: Since taking over Microsoft, Nadella has shifted the company's culture from one known for internal competition to one focused on empathy and collaboration. He articulated a clear vision of transforming Microsoft to be more about empowering others, including customers and employees. His leadership has not only led to significant financial success but also transformed Microsoft's work culture, making it more inclusive, innovative, and employee-focused.

Jacinda Ardern, Prime Minister of New Zealand: Ardern's leadership style is often highlighted for its empathetic and transparent approach, especially evident in her handling of the COVID-19 pandemic and the Christchurch mosque shootings. Her ability to articulate a vision of a united and resilient New Zealand, while showing genuine care and concern for her people, has not only brought her international acclaim but has also significantly impacted the country's social and political landscape.

Mary Barra, CEO of General Motors: Barra has been instrumental in steering General Motors through a period of significant industry change, with a clear vision of transitioning to electric and autonomous vehicles. Her leadership is characterized by a focus on safety, transparency, and inclusivity. Under her guidance, GM has not only weathered significant challenges but is also transforming into a more sustainable and innovative company.

Paul Polman, former CEO of Unilever: Polman was known for his visionary leadership at Unilever, particularly his commitment to sustainability and ethical practices. He set out a clear vision for making sustainable living commonplace and redefining business success to include social and environmental impact. His leadership transformed Unilever's strategy and operations, leading to both financial success and a notable positive impact on the environment and communities.

Sheryl Sandberg, COO of Facebook: As the COO of Facebook, Sandberg has been a proponent of building a more empathetic and transparent workplace culture. She has been vocal about issues like gender equality and work-life balance, using her platform to inspire change both within and outside of Facebook. Her leadership style and advocacy work have had a significant impact on corporate culture discussions globally.

These leaders exemplify the principles of Light Leadership, demonstrating how empathy, transparency, and a commitment to the collective well-being can drive not only business success but also positive societal change. Their visions have not only transformed their respective organizations but have also provided a roadmap for other leaders aspiring to make a meaningful impact.

Implementing Light Leadership in the workplace involves integrating its core principles – empathy, transparency, and a focus on collective well-being – into the daily operations of an organization. This process requires a strategic and consistent approach to ensure that these values are not just espoused but actively practiced and embedded in the organizational culture.

1. Start with Leadership Training: Begin by training leaders and managers in the principles of Light Leadership. This can include workshops, seminars, and coaching sessions focused on developing empathy, transparent communication, and strategies for promoting collective well-being.

2. Model the Behavior: Leaders should embody Light Leadership qualities in their daily interactions and decision-making processes. By demonstrating empathy, transparency, and a focus on well-

being in their actions, leaders set a powerful example for the rest of the organization.

3. Revise Policies and Procedures: Review and revise company policies and procedures to align with Light Leadership principles. This could involve updating communication protocols, decision-making processes, and performance evaluation criteria to emphasize empathy, transparency, and collective well-being.

4. Foster Open Communication: Create multiple channels for open and transparent communication. Encourage regular team meetings, one-on-one check-ins, and anonymous feedback mechanisms. Ensure that employees feel comfortable sharing their thoughts and know that their voices are heard and valued.

5. Prioritize Employee Well-being: Implement initiatives and programs that focus on the well-being of employees. This can include flexible working arrangements, mental health resources, wellness programs, and team-building activities that promote a healthy work-life balance and a supportive work environment.

6. Encourage Team Collaboration: Promote a collaborative work environment where team members are encouraged to work together, share ideas, and support each other. Team projects and cross-departmental collaborations can be effective ways to foster this sense of community and collective effort.

7. Recognize and Reward: Develop recognition and reward systems that acknowledge not only individual achievements but also contributions to team success and the overall well-being of the organization. Celebrate milestones and successes that align with Light Leadership values.

8. Regular Assessment and Feedback: Conduct regular assessments to gauge how well Light Leadership principles are being integrated into the workplace. Use surveys, interviews, and performance data to gather feedback and make necessary adjustments.

9. Continuous Improvement: Light Leadership is an ongoing journey, not a one-time initiative. Continuously seek ways to improve and deepen the practice of these principles in the organization. Stay open to learning and adapting as the needs of the employees and the organization evolve.

By strategically implementing these steps, an organization can effectively integrate Light Leadership principles into its daily operations, leading to a more empathetic, transparent, and supportive workplace culture. This approach not only enhances employee satisfaction and well-being but also drives organizational success and sustainability.

Overcoming challenges and resistance to change when implementing Light Leadership in the workplace is a critical step in ensuring the successful adoption of this leadership style. Change, especially in organizational culture, often meets resistance due to various reasons such as fear of the unknown, comfort with the status quo, or skepticism about the new approach.

The first step in overcoming these challenges is to understand the source of the resistance. Engage with employees at all levels to listen to their concerns and apprehensions. This not only helps in identifying the root causes of resistance but also demonstrates empathy, a key aspect of Light Leadership.

Effective communication is crucial in managing resistance to change. Clearly articulate the benefits of Light Leadership not just for the organization, but also for the employees. Illustrate how this leadership style can lead to a more positive work environment, improved job satisfaction, and better work-life balance. Transparency about the changes, how they will be implemented, and the expected outcomes can alleviate fears and uncertainties. Involving employees in the change process can significantly reduce resistance. When employees are part of the decision-making process, they are more likely to feel a sense of ownership and commitment to the change. Create opportunities for employees to provide input and feedback throughout the implementation process.

Provide adequate training and support to help employees transition to the new way of working. This could include workshops, mentoring, and access to resources that help them understand and adapt to Light Leadership principles.

Demonstrating quick wins can also be effective in overcoming resistance. Identify areas where changes can be implemented relatively easily and show immediate benefits. This helps in building momentum and convincing skeptics about the value of the new leadership approach.

Leadership commitment is essential in overcoming resistance. Leaders at all levels should consistently demonstrate the behaviors and practices associated with Light Leadership. This sets a precedent and signals to employees that the change is important and here to stay. Be patient and persistent. Cultural change is a gradual process and requires time. Continuously reinforce the importance of Light Leadership, celebrate milestones, and remain committed to the vision.

By addressing the root causes of resistance, involving employees in the process, communicating effectively, providing support, demonstrating quick wins, and showing commitment from leadership, organizations can successfully overcome challenges and resistance, paving the way for a successful adoption of Light Leadership.

Balancing empathy with decisiveness and direction is an essential aspect of Light Leadership, ensuring that while leaders are understanding and considerate of their team's emotions and perspectives, they also maintain clear goals and make firm decisions when necessary.

To achieve this balance, it's important to first establish a clear vision and set of objectives for the team or organization. This direction serves as a guiding star for all decision-making processes and actions. When this vision is clear, it's easier to make decisions that align with these goals, even when they are tough.

At the same time, empathy plays a crucial role in how these decisions are communicated and implemented. When making decisions, consider how they will impact the team not just on a professional level but also on a personal level. Communicate decisions in a way that shows understanding and consideration for how they might affect the team members.

One effective approach is to involve the team in the decision-making process. While the final decision may rest with the leader, soliciting input and feedback from the team can provide valuable insights and help them feel valued and understood. This participative approach can enhance buy-in and ease the implementation of decisions.

However, there will be times when quick, decisive action is needed, without the possibility of extensive team consultation. In these instances, it's important for a leader to confidently make a decision and then communicate it transparently, explaining the reasoning behind it and how it aligns with the overall vision and goals.

After making decisions, be open to feedback and be willing to adjust if necessary. This flexibility demonstrates that while you are decisive, you are also empathetic to the outcomes of your decisions and willing to make changes for the betterment of the team and the organization.

Demonstrating empathy doesn't mean avoiding difficult conversations or decisions. It means handling them in a way that is respectful, considerate, and understanding. It's about ensuring that even when tough choices are made, team members feel supported and respected throughout the process.

Balancing empathy with decisiveness and direction involves being clear about your goals and vision, involving your team in the decision-making process, communicating decisions with empathy and transparency, and being flexible and responsive to feedback. This balanced approach enables leaders to guide their teams effectively while maintaining a supportive and understanding work environment.

Measuring the impact of Light Leadership involves evaluating how this leadership style influences team dynamics, employee morale, and overall productivity. It's crucial to use a combination of qualitative and quantitative methods to gain a comprehensive understanding of its effectiveness.

1. Employee Surveys and Feedback

Conduct regular employee surveys to gauge satisfaction, engagement, and morale. Include questions that specifically assess aspects of Light Leadership, such as perceived empathy, transparency, and focus on well-being from management. Implement feedback tools like suggestion boxes or digital platforms where employees can anonymously share their thoughts about leadership and workplace culture.

2. Performance Metrics:

Analyze productivity and performance metrics before and after implementing Light Leadership practices. Look for changes in key performance indicators (KPIs), such as sales figures, project completion rates, or customer satisfaction scores. Assess employee retention rates and absenteeism. Improvements in these areas can indicate a more positive work environment under Light Leadership.

3. One-on-One Interviews and Exit Interviews:

Conduct regular one-on-one interviews with employees to get deeper insights into their experiences with Light Leadership. Utilize exit interviews to understand the reasons behind employees leaving the organization and to gather feedback on leadership and company culture.

4. 360-Degree Feedback:

Implement 360-degree feedback systems that allow employees to provide feedback on their leaders. This can offer valuable insights into how Light Leadership practices are perceived across different levels of the organization.

5. Observation and Informal Conversations:

Leaders and HR personnel can observe team interactions and listen to informal conversations to get a sense of the workplace atmosphere. Casual interactions with employees can provide anecdotal evidence of the impact of Light Leadership practices.

6. Focus Groups:

Conduct focus groups with employees from various departments to discuss their perceptions of leadership and workplace culture. This can provide qualitative data on the effectiveness of Light Leadership practices.

7. Wellness and Well-being Assessments:

Use wellness surveys or tools to assess the mental and physical health of employees, as a focus on well-being is a key component of Light Leadership.

8. Customer Feedback:

Evaluate customer feedback and reviews, as improvements in customer satisfaction can often be linked to better employee morale and effective leadership.

A combination of direct feedback methods, performance analysis, and observational techniques provides a robust framework for measuring the impact of Light Leadership. These methods can help leaders understand the strengths and areas for improvement in their approach and guide further development of their leadership style.

Emphasizing the need for ongoing learning and growth as a leader is integral to the journey of Light Leadership. In an ever-evolving business landscape, continuous learning is not just beneficial; it's essential for maintaining effective leadership. This commitment to growth ensures that leaders stay adaptable, resilient, and capable of meeting new challenges.

Ongoing learning involves staying abreast of industry trends, leadership theories, and organizational best practices. This might mean attending workshops, seminars, and conferences, or engaging in formal education such as leadership courses or advanced degrees. It also includes staying informed about broader socio-economic developments that can impact your organization and team.

Growth as a leader extends beyond formal learning. It encompasses seeking and reflecting on feedback from peers, superiors, and team members. This feedback provides invaluable insights into areas of strength and opportunities for improvement. Engaging in reflective practices, such as journaling or coaching sessions, allows leaders to introspect and grow from their experiences. Networking with other leaders and professionals provides a platform for sharing experiences, challenges, and strategies. These interactions can offer new perspectives and ideas, contributing to a leader's growth and adaptability.

Personal development is another crucial aspect of ongoing learning. This involves developing emotional intelligence, honing communication skills, and cultivating a mindset open to change and innovation. It also means learning to balance professional responsibilities with personal well-being, as a leader's personal health directly impacts their professional effectiveness.

Fostering a culture of learning within the organization is a reflection of a leader's commitment to growth. Encouraging team members to pursue their professional and personal development not only enhances the organization's capabilities but also demonstrates the leader's dedication to collective improvement and success.

Ongoing learning and growth is about adopting a mindset of continuous improvement and adaptability. It's recognizing that leadership is a journey, not a destination, and that the most effective leaders are those who continually seek to enhance their knowledge, skills, and personal well-being.

Adapting one's leadership style to different situations and challenges is essential for effective leadership, especially in the realm of Light Leadership which values empathy, transparency, and collective well-being. A leader's ability to flexibly shift their approach depending on the specific demands of each scenario is a valuable skill.

It begins with a deep understanding of the situation at hand. Assessing the nuances, stakeholders involved, and potential outcomes is crucial. Depending on whether the situation is a crisis, a routine operation, or a change initiative, different leadership approaches are required. For instance, in high-stress situations, a more supportive and understanding approach might be necessary, while in times of change, a directive approach could be more effective.

Leaders should be comfortable moving along the spectrum of leadership styles. A democratic style may be suitable in situations where diverse ideas and team input are valuable, whereas an autocratic style may be more effective when quick decisions are needed. This flexibility ensures that leaders can respond effectively to a variety of challenges.

Adapting communication style is also essential. Crisis situations might call for more direct and clear communication, while collaborative projects could benefit from an open and inclusive approach. The ability to tailor communication to the situation helps in ensuring messages are effectively conveyed and understood.

Cultural sensitivity is another important aspect of adaptive leadership. In globally diverse teams, understanding and respecting cultural differences is key to effective leadership. What works in one cultural context might not be suitable in another, so adapting one's style to these differences is vital.

Reflecting on the effectiveness of the adapted leadership style is important, and this is where feedback from team members and colleagues becomes invaluable. Continuous learning and adaptation from each experience refine a leader's ability to effectively switch their approach.

Leaders also need to develop resilience to manage stress and maintain clear decision-making in various circumstances. This personal resilience is critical for navigating the complexities of different leadership scenarios.

Lastly, engaging in ongoing leadership development is beneficial. Exposure to different leadership theories and models through training, mentoring, or self-study provides a diverse set of strategies and techniques that leaders can draw upon as needed.

The journey to becoming a Light Leader, as detailed in this chapter, is a multifaceted process that combines personal development, strategic implementation, and a deep commitment to the core values of empathy, transparency, and collective well-being. This journey is not a linear path but an ongoing cycle of learning, application, and adaptation.

Initially, it involves a deep introspection to understand and embrace the principles of Light Leadership. This means cultivating a mindset that prioritizes understanding and connecting with team members, fostering open and honest communication, and consistently working towards the happiness and success of the team.

A critical part of this journey is developing self-awareness. Leaders are encouraged to engage in self-assessment tools and reflective practices to understand their strengths and areas for improvement. This self-awareness is crucial in effectively applying the principles of Light Leadership in various situations.

The chapter emphasizes the importance of empathy in leadership. Developing and nurturing empathy involves actively listening to and genuinely understanding the perspectives and needs of team members. This quality helps in building trust and strong relationships, which are fundamental to Light Leadership.

Another key aspect of the journey is learning to balance empathy with decisiveness and direction. Leaders are guided to adapt their leadership style to different situations while maintaining a clear vision and objectives. This balance ensures that while leaders are considerate and understanding, they also provide firm guidance and direction to their teams.

Implementing Light Leadership in the workplace requires a strategic approach. Leaders are encouraged to integrate Light Leadership principles into daily operations, overcome challenges and resistance to change, and measure the impact of their leadership style on team morale and productivity.

The chapter also underscores the need for ongoing learning and growth as a leader. Embracing continuous development, staying adaptable to changing situations, and remaining committed to the principles of Light Leadership are crucial for sustained effectiveness in this role.

The journey to becoming a Light Leader is a transformative process that requires commitment, self-awareness, and a dedication to fostering a positive and productive work environment. It's a journey marked by continuous learning, empathy, and a commitment to leading in a way that elevates both individuals and the organization as a whole.

The enduring value of enlightened leadership in the modern world is increasingly evident. In an era characterized by rapid change, complex challenges, and a greater emphasis on ethical practices and social responsibility, the principles of enlightened leadership are not just beneficial but essential.

Enlightened leadership, which encompasses empathy, transparency, and a focus on collective well-being, offers a path forward that aligns with the evolving values and expectations of today's workforce and society. This leadership style recognizes the importance of treating employees not just as workers but as whole individuals with diverse needs and aspirations. By prioritizing empathy, enlightened leaders create a work environment where employees feel valued and understood, leading to higher engagement, creativity, and productivity.

Transparency in leadership fosters trust and respect, both within the organization and with external stakeholders. In a world where information is readily available, and accountability is demanded, being open and honest in business practices is not just morally right but also strategically smart. Transparency builds a strong reputation and loyal customer base, which are invaluable assets in a competitive market.

The focus on collective well-being under enlightened leadership extends beyond the confines of the organization. It encompasses a broader responsibility towards society and the environment, recognizing that businesses have a role to play in creating a sustainable and equitable world. This approach aligns with the increasing consumer and employee demand for socially responsible and environmentally conscious business practices.

The ability of enlightened leaders to adapt and lead through complex and uncertain situations is invaluable. The modern world, with its rapid technological advancements and global interconnectedness, requires leaders who can navigate these complexities with foresight and agility.

The enduring value of enlightened leadership lies in its ability to meet the needs of the present while preparing for the challenges of the future. It presents a leadership model that is not only effective in achieving business success but also in contributing positively to the well-being of employees, communities, and the broader environment. As the world continues to evolve, the principles of enlightened leadership will remain relevant and crucial for creating a sustainable, ethical, and prosperous future.

Conclusion: "The Leadership Spectrum: From Sith to Saint"

In this conclusion to "From Dark to Light Leadership," we reflect on the transformative journey from destructive, imbalanced leadership to a more enlightened, positive approach. This journey, as explored in the book, reveals the profound impact that leadership styles have on both individuals and organizations. We have journeyed through the shadowy realms of 'Darth Vader in a Suit', balanced the scales in 'The Zen Masters', and aspired to the ideals of 'The Gandhi of the Boardroom'. Now, as we synthesize these insights, we aim to empower leaders with the tools and wisdom to foster environments of growth, harmony, and sustainable success. This concluding section will not only tie together key themes but also provide a roadmap for leaders aspiring to make a meaningful, positive change in their spheres of influence.

This chapter serves as an integrative wrap-up, contrasting the diverse approaches to leadership - from the autocratic 'Sith' styles, characterized by control and authority, to the enlightened 'Saint' styles, marked by empathy and inclusivity.

We embark on a reflective journey, revisiting the key leadership styles examined in previous chapters, drawing contrasts and comparisons to paint a comprehensive picture of the leadership spectrum. The purpose here is not just to reiterate what has been learned, but to synthesize these insights, highlighting how each style has its unique place and value in different organizational contexts.

This chapter explores the dynamics and complexities of leadership. It acknowledges that there's no one-size-fits-all approach, but rather a fluid continuum where styles can be adapted and blended according to the needs of the team, the organizational culture, and the specific challenges faced.

By integrating these diverse styles, the chapter aims to provide a final, holistic view of leadership, equipping readers with a broad understanding of how they can apply these lessons to their own leadership journeys. Whether you see yourself as a 'Sith' or a 'Saint' or somewhere in between, this chapter will offer valuable insights into harnessing your unique leadership style for the greatest impact.

As we reach the conclusion of our exploration into the multifaceted world of leadership, it's essential to reflect on the journey through the various leadership styles we have encountered. Each style, with its unique characteristics and approaches, provides valuable lessons and insights into the art of effective leadership.

Authoritative Leadership: We began with the traditional, authoritative style, where decision-making is centralized, and control is paramount. This style, often necessary in crisis situations, emphasizes clear direction and quick decision-making but risks stifling creativity and disengaging employees.

Transactional Leadership: We examined transactional leadership, which operates on a system of rewards and penalties. Effective in achieving short-term goals, this style can be limiting for innovation and long-term commitment.

Transformational Leadership: In contrast, transformational leadership focuses on inspiring and motivating employees to exceed expectations. This style fosters a passionate and energetic work environment but requires leaders to be charismatic and visionary.

Servant Leadership: Servant leadership, which prioritizes the growth and well-being of team members, emerged as a powerful model for creating supportive and inclusive workplaces. It challenges conventional leadership norms by putting the needs of employees first.

Participative Leadership: The participative or democratic style, which values the input and collaboration of team members in decision-making, was explored for its ability to foster a sense of ownership and engagement among employees.

Situational Leadership: We delved into situational leadership, which adapts to the changing needs of the team and individual members. This flexible approach requires leaders to be perceptive and responsive to their environment.

Ethical and Moral Leadership: The importance of ethical and moral leadership was underscored, highlighting how integrity and ethical considerations are crucial in today's business world.

Innovative and Adaptive Leadership: We looked at innovative and adaptive leadership styles, essential in today's fast-paced, constantly changing business landscape. These styles emphasize creativity, flexibility, and resilience.

Light Leadership: Finally, we explored Light Leadership, a style that combines empathy, transparency, and a focus on collective well-being. This contemporary approach responds to the evolving demands of the modern workforce, emphasizing emotional intelligence and social responsibility.

"The Dark Side of Leadership: Sith Lords of the Boardroom" was a crucial chapter that scrutinized authoritarian leadership styles, likening them to 'Sith Lords' from fictional narratives. This segment delved into the characteristics and impacts of such leadership, marked by dominance and fear. It discussed how these leaders create oppressive work environments, negatively affecting employee morale, stifling innovation, and leading to high turnover rates. This chapter was instrumental in understanding the destructive effects of authoritarian leadership on both the organizational health and the well-being of employees.

In the book, the section on authoritative, control-based leadership styles examined leaders who prioritized power and order, often valuing obedience over creativity and flexibility. It highlighted the creation of rigid organizational structures where decisions were top-down, with little room for employee input. These leaders maintained strict control, enforcing rules often at the expense of a healthy workplace culture. This approach led to environments where innovation was stifled, and employee well-being was not a priority, illustrating the downsides of such leadership styles.

We provided extensive examples and characteristics of 'Sith Lord' leaders, illustrating their authoritarian, control-based leadership style. These leaders were portrayed as prioritizing power and control, often ruling through fear and intimidation. Characteristics included a lack of empathy, resistance to feedback, and a focus on personal gain over team or organizational success. These leaders often created environments where dissent was not tolerated and conformity was enforced, leading to a culture of fear and suppressed innovation. The examples highlighted the detrimental effects such leaders have on both employees and organizational health, underscoring the importance of recognizing and addressing these destructive leadership styles.

The impact of authoritarian leadership on organizations and employees was explored in depth. Such leadership often leads to a stifling work environment, where fear and compliance overshadow creativity and collaboration. Employees under these regimes experience high levels of stress and job dissatisfaction, resulting in decreased productivity and higher turnover rates. Organizations suffer as well, with a lack of innovation, damaged reputations, and potential long-term financial and operational setbacks. This analysis highlighted the critical need for leadership that supports and empowers employees rather than dominating them.

The transition from authoritative to more democratic and inclusive leadership styles is a significant shift in organizational management. This change reflects an evolving understanding of what drives employee engagement and organizational success.

Initially, authoritative leadership was predominant. Here, decisions were made at the top and cascaded down. This approach often led to a lack of employee involvement in decision-making, resulting in disengagement and a lack of creativity.

As the drawbacks of this style became evident, there was a gradual shift towards more democratic and inclusive approaches. These styles emphasize collaboration, employee participation in decision-making, and a more open communication culture. Such environments encourage diverse ideas and foster a sense of ownership among employees, leading to increased motivation and productivity.

Inclusive leadership is characterized by its focus on valuing and leveraging the diverse backgrounds and perspectives of all team members. It's about creating an environment where everyone feels respected and empowered to contribute their best work.

The evolution to more democratic and inclusive leadership styles signify a deeper understanding of the complex dynamics of modern organizations and the diverse needs of their workforce. It represents a move towards creating more sustainable, innovative, and people-centric workplaces.

Several factors have influenced the transition from authoritative to more democratic and inclusive leadership styles in the real world:

Globalization and Diversity: The increasing diversity in the workforce and globalized business operations have necessitated more inclusive leadership styles to cater to diverse needs and perspectives.

Technological Advancements: Technology has democratized information access, empowering employees with knowledge and tools, thereby encouraging a more collaborative environment.

Changing Workforce Expectations: Modern employees, especially younger generations, prefer workplaces that value their input and foster a sense of belonging.

Research and Evidence: Studies showing the benefits of inclusive and democratic leadership on employee satisfaction and productivity have influenced this shift.

Increased Focus on Ethics and Corporate Social Responsibility: There's a growing expectation for organizations to be ethically and socially responsible, which aligns well with more inclusive leadership styles.

Competitive Advantage: Organizations have recognized that inclusive leadership can be a source of competitive advantage, leading to innovation and better decision-making.

The journey of a leader through various leadership styles over time is a reflective and evolutionary process. Initially, leaders might gravitate towards an authoritative style, characterized by a top-down approach and centralized decision-making. This stage often mirrors their early career mindset, focused on establishing authority and driving results swiftly.

As leaders progress, they encounter diverse situations and workforce demographics, prompting a reevaluation of their leadership style. Exposure to different perspectives and the complexities of managing varied teams catalyzes a shift towards more inclusive and democratic approaches. This phase is marked by a growing appreciation for collaborative decision-making, where the leader values and integrates the input of team members.

This evolution is further influenced by the changing dynamics of the business world, where adaptability and innovation become key to success. Leaders recognize that fostering a culture of openness and empowerment not only enhances employee satisfaction but also drives creativity and problem-solving. This realization leads to a more empathetic and ethical leadership approach, focusing on the growth and well-being of both individuals and the organization. Over time, this journey transforms leaders into facilitators and mentors, who prioritize building a supportive and engaging work environment. They become champions of diversity and inclusion, understanding that a multitude of perspectives enriches decision-making and organizational culture. The leadership spectrum journey is a continuous process of learning, adapting, and embracing change, reflecting a leader's personal growth and the evolving needs of the modern workplace.

"Balanced Leadership: The Jedi Approach" presents a leadership style that seamlessly combines elements of authority with empathy and teamwork. It describes leaders who, much like the Jedi, strike a balance between assertiveness and understanding. These leaders recognize the importance of firm decision-making, when necessary, yet remain open to feedback and diverse perspectives. By valuing and integrating team members' input, they foster a workplace environment where respect and collaboration are paramount. This approach leads to a healthy, productive organizational culture, marked by balanced decision-making and inclusive practices. This Jedi-like leadership style exemplifies the blend of various leadership qualities to achieve the best outcomes for both the organization and its people.

Drawing parallels to the Jedi philosophy in "Balanced Leadership: The Jedi Approach," leaders are seen as embodying wisdom, balance, and a focus on the greater good. This approach is about applying wisdom in decision-making, considering the broader implications of actions rather than just immediate gains. Balance is key, with leaders avoiding extremes in management styles, thereby creating a harmonious work environment. The commitment to the greater good is paramount, with decisions aimed at benefiting the team and organization holistically. This leadership style encourages ethical practices, fosters trust, and promotes long-term success, reflecting the Jedi's dedication to harmony and moral integrity.

The middle-ground approach of balanced leadership offers several advantages and challenges. It creates a more engaged and motivated workforce, as employees feel valued and heard. This approach also fosters a more adaptable and innovative environment, as diverse perspectives are considered in decision-making. However, finding the right balance can be challenging, as it requires constant adjustment and sensitivity to various situations and team dynamics. Additionally, this style may sometimes lead to slower decision-making processes, as it involves gathering and considering multiple viewpoints.

A leader's development into a balanced, Jedi-like figure is a journey of self-awareness and adaptation. It starts with understanding one's own leadership style and its impacts. Through experiences, feedback, and introspection, leaders learn to incorporate empathy, open-mindedness, and ethical decision-making. This growth involves learning to value diverse perspectives and fostering an inclusive environment. The journey is continuous, requiring ongoing effort to maintain balance between different leadership aspects, while focusing on the greater good and personal development, much like the path of a Jedi seeking harmony and wisdom.

In "The Enlightened Ones: Saints of the Corporate World," we discussed leaders who exemplify the highest ethical standards in the corporate environment. These leaders were portrayed as embodying integrity, empathy, and a strong moral compass, focusing on the well-being of their employees and the broader community. The section highlighted their commitment to ethical practices, sustainable business strategies, and creating a positive impact, contrasting sharply with earlier discussions of authoritarian leadership styles.

The 'Saint' end of the leadership spectrum, emphasizes compassionate, empathetic, and morally driven leadership. This section delved into how such leaders prioritize empathy and compassion in their interactions and decision-making, ensuring that their actions align with a strong moral compass. We explored the impact of this leadership style on creating a positive and nurturing work environment, emphasizing the well-being of employees and the ethical considerations in business practices. This approach starkly contrasts with authoritarian styles, showcasing a leadership model deeply rooted in moral integrity and human-centric values.

We presented examples of 'Saint' leaders, illustrating the positive outcomes of their compassionate and moral approach. These leaders were characterized by their empathy, ethical decision-making, and dedication to the welfare of their employees and communities. We highlighted how their leadership resulted in high employee morale, increased trust, and a strong sense of loyalty and community within the organization. This approach also often led to sustainable business practices and a positive brand image, showcasing the far-reaching benefits of moral and empathetic leadership.

The 'Saint' leadership style, focused on compassion and morality, fosters innovation by creating an environment of trust and openness, where employees feel safe to express and explore new ideas. This leadership style builds loyalty through genuine care for employee well-being and ethical practices, leading to a committed workforce. Long-term success is achieved by establishing a sustainable and positive brand reputation, attracting talent and customers who value ethical practices, and nurturing a work culture that supports continuous improvement and adaptability.

In "From Dark to Light Leadership," we explored how various leadership styles, from Sith-like authoritarian to saint-like empathetic, impact organizational outcomes. Authoritative styles, while efficient, often create rigid, fear-based environments, stifling creativity and morale. In contrast, balanced, Jedi-like leadership fosters collaboration, innovation, and employee satisfaction, albeit with challenges in decision-making speed. Enlightened, saint-like leadership promotes ethical practices, high morale, and sustainable success, though it requires balancing idealism with practical business needs. These styles illustrate the profound effect leadership can have on an organization's culture and performance.

We also analyzed how different leadership styles historically impacted organizational culture, employee satisfaction, and business success. Authoritative styles, likened to 'Sith Lords', were found to create a culture of fear, negatively affecting employee morale and stifling innovation. In contrast, balanced leadership, akin to the 'Jedi' approach, was associated with a positive culture, higher employee satisfaction, and a nurturing environment for innovation. Finally, the 'Saint' leadership style, characterized by compassion and ethical focus, was shown to greatly enhance organizational culture and employee well-being, contributing to sustainable business success and a positive brand image.

We discussed how various factors such as industry, company size, and culture influence a leader's position on the leadership spectrum. It emphasizes that there is no one-size-fits-all approach to leadership, as different contexts require different styles. For instance, a startup might benefit more from a flexible, democratic style, while a large, established corporation might need a more structured approach. The book underlines the importance of leaders being adaptable and aware of their specific organizational context to effectively manage and lead.

Indeed, in light of the influence of context on leadership styles, the adaptability of leaders to different environments becomes paramount. Leaders must possess the ability to flexibly adjust their leadership approach based on the unique needs and challenges of their organization and industry. This adaptability is a key trait of effective leaders as it allows them to navigate diverse situations successfully.

For instance, a leader who can transition from a democratic, inclusive style in a creative industry to a more authoritative approach in a highly regulated sector demonstrates adaptability. They understand that what works in one context may not be effective in another and are willing to tailor their leadership style to achieve the best outcomes. This adaptability not only enhances the leader's effectiveness but also contributes to organizational success by aligning leadership with the specific demands of the environment.

Future leaders will need to be even more adaptable and open to change as the business landscape continues to evolve. The rise of technology and remote work, for example, may require leaders to develop new skills in digital leadership and virtual team management. There's an anticipation that leadership styles will increasingly prioritize ethics, social responsibility, and employee well-being. Leaders will be expected to lead with a strong moral compass and consider the broader societal impact of their decisions.

The section on the future of leadership also suggests that diversity and inclusion will play a more significant role in leadership styles. Leaders will need to create environments that celebrate diversity and harness the power of different perspectives for innovation and success. The future of leadership will demand leaders who are agile, ethical, and inclusive, capable of navigating a rapidly changing world while prioritizing the well-being and growth of their employees and organizations.

The growing importance of ethical and empathetic leadership in modern business was a central theme. We highlighted how the business landscape is evolving to place a significant emphasis on leaders who prioritize ethics and empathy. Ethical leadership has become crucial due to increased scrutiny and public awareness of corporate practices. Leaders who operate with a strong moral compass are better equipped to make decisions that align with societal values and avoid ethical pitfalls. This not only enhances the reputation of the organization but also fosters trust among stakeholders.

Empathetic leadership is also gaining prominence as organizations recognize the value of employee well-being and morale. Leaders who demonstrate empathy are better at understanding and addressing the needs of their teams. This leads to higher employee satisfaction, increased productivity, and reduced turnover rates. In a world characterized by rapid change and uncertainty, empathetic leaders can provide stability and support to their teams, helping them navigate challenges effectively. The book underscores that ethical and empathetic leadership is no longer a nice-to-have but a fundamental requirement for modern businesses to thrive in an increasingly interconnected and socially conscious world.

Encouraging leaders to be dynamic and evolve along the leadership spectrum is a crucial message we want to convey. It emphasizes that effective leadership is not a fixed position but a continuous journey of growth and adaptation. Leaders are encouraged to assess their current leadership styles and remain open to change based on the evolving needs of their organizations and the broader context.

The book advocates for leaders to be flexible in their approach, shifting between authoritative, balanced, and empathetic styles as circumstances require. It highlights that successful leaders recognize when to assert authority, when to collaborate, and when to prioritize empathy. We encourage leaders to invest in their personal development, including acquiring new skills and honing their emotional intelligence. By doing so, leaders can better navigate the complexities of modern business and lead their teams to success. The message is that leaders should be agile and willing to adapt their leadership styles to optimize organizational outcomes, ensuring that they remain effective and relevant in an ever-changing business landscape.

We encourage readers to engage in introspection and self-improvement regarding their own leadership styles. Our book emphasized the significance of self-reflection, urging individuals to assess their existing leadership approaches and determine whether they leaned more towards authoritative, balanced, or empathetic styles. Through this process of self-reflection, they gained valuable insights into their strengths and areas for improvement as leaders.

The book underscored the importance of continuous personal growth. It advocated for leaders to invest in their own development, whether through formal education, mentorship, or self-improvement initiatives. By consistently honing their leadership skills and expanding their knowledge, individuals became more effective and adaptable leaders.

The book provides valuable tips for personal growth and movement along the leadership spectrum, encouraging individuals to become more dynamic and adaptable leaders:

1. Self-Reflection: Begin by assessing your current leadership style. Reflect on whether you tend to be authoritative, balanced, or empathetic in your approach. Understanding your starting point is essential for growth.

2. Continuous Learning: Invest in your personal development through continuous learning. Seek opportunities for formal education, attend leadership workshops, and read books on leadership to expand your knowledge and skills.

3. Mentorship: Consider finding a mentor or coach who can provide guidance and feedback on your leadership journey. Learning from someone with more experience can be invaluable.

4. Feedback: Actively seek feedback from your team members and colleagues. Constructive feedback can help you identify areas for improvement and adjust your leadership style accordingly.

5. Flexibility: Embrace flexibility and adaptability in your leadership. Recognize that different situations may require different approaches. Be willing to transition between authoritative, balanced, and empathetic styles as needed.

6. Empathy and Emotional Intelligence: Develop your emotional intelligence and empathy. Understanding the emotions and perspectives of others can enhance your ability to lead with compassion and effectiveness.

7. Lead by Example: Model the behaviors and values you want to see in your team. Be a role model for ethical conduct, collaboration, and empathy.

8. Set Clear Goals: Define clear leadership goals and objectives. Having a vision for your leadership journey will guide your efforts and provide a sense of direction.

9. Regular Self-Assessment: Periodically assess your progress along the leadership spectrum. Are you evolving in your leadership style? Are you achieving the desired outcomes?

10. Seek Inspiration: Look to leaders you admire for inspiration. Study their leadership journeys and the strategies they employed to become effective leaders.

By following these tips, individuals can embark on a path of personal growth and transformation, gradually evolving and adapting their leadership styles to become dynamic and effective leaders in a variety of contexts.

The book strongly emphasizes the paramount importance of self-awareness and continuous learning in leadership development. These two factors serve as foundational pillars for individuals seeking to evolve and excel as leaders.

Self-awareness entails recognizing one's own strengths, weaknesses, values, and biases. It is a critical aspect of leadership as it enables leaders to understand how their actions, decisions, and communication impact those around them. Being self-aware allows leaders to identify areas for improvement in their leadership style, recognize the impact of their leadership on organizational culture and employee satisfaction, and make necessary adjustments to align with their leadership goals.

On the other hand, continuous learning is essential for leaders to stay relevant and effective. Leadership is not a static skill but an ongoing journey of growth and adaptation. Continuous learning involves seeking new knowledge and skills through education and training, learning from experiences (both successes and failures), and keeping up with industry trends and best practices.

Leaders who prioritize self-awareness and continuous learning are better equipped to adapt to changing circumstances and industry demands. They can understand and connect with their teams on a deeper level, identify and rectify leadership blind spots, and ultimately lead with authenticity and empathy. These qualities contribute to organizational success and personal growth, making self-awareness and continuous learning fundamental in the development of effective leaders.

Wrapping up the concepts and insights from the book, we've delved into a comprehensive exploration of leadership styles, from authoritative and control-based approaches reminiscent of 'Sith Lords' to balanced and empathetic leadership akin to 'Jedi,' and finally, the ethical and compassionate 'Saint' leaders.

Throughout our journey, we've discussed how these various leadership styles impact organizational culture, employee satisfaction, and business success. We've emphasized the significance of context in shaping leadership styles, recognizing that adaptability is key for leaders to thrive in diverse environments.

The book has also underscored the growing importance of ethical and empathetic leadership in modern business, emphasizing the need for leaders to prioritize ethics and employee well-being. We've encouraged leaders to be dynamic and adaptable, continuously evolving along the leadership spectrum. Personal reflection and growth have been highlighted as essential steps in this journey, urging individuals to assess their leadership styles and invest in their personal development.

We've touched upon the predictions for the future of leadership, anticipating that leaders will need to be agile, ethical, and inclusive to navigate the evolving business landscape successfully. The book has stressed the significance of self-awareness and continuous learning in leadership development, recognizing them as foundational elements for effective leadership. We have offered a comprehensive roadmap for individuals aspiring to become dynamic, adaptable, and effective leaders, urging them to prioritize ethics, empathy, and personal growth on their leadership journey.

Final thoughts on the diverse nature of leadership underscore the recognition that leadership is not a one-size-fits-all concept. Instead, it is a dynamic and multifaceted discipline that evolves based on the context, challenges, and goals of an organization. The book has demonstrated that leadership can take on various forms, ranging from authoritative to balanced and empathetic styles.

The diverse nature of leadership is a reflection of the complex and ever-changing world of business. It acknowledges that leaders must adapt their styles to meet the unique demands of their organizations, industries, and teams. What works in one situation may not be effective in another, and successful leaders are those who can navigate this diversity with skill and agility.

The book has highlighted the ethical imperative in leadership, emphasizing the growing importance of ethics, empathy, and moral values in modern business. Leaders are increasingly expected to consider the broader impact of their decisions and prioritize the well-being of their employees and communities. The diverse nature of leadership celebrates the richness and complexity of this field, recognizing that effective leaders are those who can flexibly adapt their styles, prioritize ethics and empathy, and continuously grow and learn on their leadership journey. It is a reminder that leadership is not a destination but a dynamic and ever-evolving path toward success and positive impact.

In closing, we encourage leaders to embark on a journey of self-discovery and leadership excellence by finding their unique position on the 'Leadership Spectrum.' This spectrum encompasses wisdom, balance, empathy, and strength, and it offers a dynamic range of leadership styles to draw from.

Leaders, you are not bound to a single point on this spectrum; rather, you have the power to navigate and blend these qualities to suit the diverse needs of your organization and teams. Seek wisdom in your decisions, balance in your approach, empathy in your interactions, and strength in your resolve.

Remember that leadership is not a static state but an ongoing evolution. Embrace the challenges and opportunities that come your way, and be willing to adapt, learn, and grow. As you find your unique place on the Leadership Spectrum, you will not only lead with authenticity and impact but also inspire those around you to do the same.

In this ever-changing world of business, your ability to blend wisdom, balance, empathy, and strength will be your compass, guiding you towards leadership excellence and a positive legacy. Embrace the journey and let your leadership shine as a beacon of inspiration for others to follow.